Illustrations **ALAN BERRY RHYS** ★ ★ ★ ★ ★ ★ ★ *Author* **HEATHER ALEXANDER**

WEIRD
AND
Wonderful

THE UNITED STATES IS LIKE NOWHERE ELSE ON THE PLANET. There are bustling cities, tropical beaches, rocky coastlines, snow-capped mountains, thick forests, windswept deserts, and rich farmland. The country boasts a vast and varied landscape and a "melting pot" of people. Immigrants from all over the world, in addition to the Indigenous nations, call the U.S. home. This unique jumble of geography and people has given each of the 50 states (and the nation's capital, Washington, D.C.) its own distinct personality and quirks.

Inside this book, we highlight the supersized objects, off-beat collections, head-scratching history, wacky world records, and incredible natural wonders from coast to coast. We honor each state's oddball ingenuity and bizarre engineering feats. And we showcase the strangest monuments, quirkiest museums, and silliest festivals you never knew existed. (Trust us, there's a community out there that shares your same fondness for a particular food or unusual hobby!). In addition to the *WEIRD*, we celebrate the *WONDERFUL*—the people and groups whose bravery and contributions to the nation make you say "wow!"

Join us on a wacky road trip around the U.S., as we explore the unexpected, the funny, the awe-inspiring, and the amazing. **THE *WEIRD* AND *WONDERFUL* UNITED STATES AWAITS!**

The Yellowhammer State
BAMA

What's in the Book

STATE NICKNAME(S)
Some state nicknames are official and some are unofficial. Some states may have more than one nickname. Usually the nickname is based on a natural feature, plant, animal, location, or something that happened there in history.

On each spread, you'll find lots of fantastic *FESTIVALS*, memorable *MUSEUMS* and *MONUMENTS*, legendary *LANDMARKS*, amazing *ANIMALS*, spectacular *SPORTS*, and remarkable *RECORD HOLDERS*.

STATE FAVORITES
Favorites, be it pizza topping or breakfast food, differ from state to state. We choose what came out on top in popularity polls, so while some selections may not be your favorites, they seem to be the favorite for the majority of people in that state.

IN **FASTFACTS** YOU'LL FIND:

STATE CAPITAL
(Every state book needs to list 'em!) This is the city with the state's government buildings.

FUNNY PLACE NAMES
On a road trip, you've probably seen signs with place names that made you chuckle. You may live in one of those places yourself! We've chosen some of the funniest ones in each state.

STATE SLANG
Ever had a friend or family member from a different state say something you'd never heard before? SLANG is a word or phrase that's unique to a certain region. Here's a mini-dictionary so you can talk-the-talk like a local.

STATE QUARTER
From 1999 to 2009, the United States Mint (the organization that makes the nation's money) circulated a quarter to honor each state and the nation's capital. We take a look at the featured symbols on each coin.

FANTASTIC FOODS
Whether putting a spin on the nation's great eats, creating original recipes with local ingredients, or sharing specialties introduced by immigrants, each state is famous for mouth-watering foods. We've listed some yummy menus.

COOL INVENTIONS
Before the invention of the wheel, everything was a drag. (That's a little invention humor for you!) We've rounded up one or two of the most pivotal inventions from each state, plus wacky facts that roll along with them.

BOOKS
A great way to "visit" a place is by reading a book! We've chosen two great titles per state. The stories are not necessarily about the state, but are set in the state. Most of the books are written for ages 7–12. We're sure you have others to add!

BY THE NUMBERS

• The U.S. is one of very few countries that write the DATE in month/day/year order.

• In short MEASURE . . . the U.S., Myanmar, and Liberia are the only three countries that haven't officially adopted the metric system.

• The U.S. has 41,704 ZIP codes, but one's top secret! Every president and first family are assigned a SECRET ZIP CODE to receive personal mail at the White House.

• The U.S. has NO OFFICIAL LANGUAGE. More than 350 languages are spoken or signed.

• More than 11,000 AMENDMENTS to the U.S. Constitution have been proposed, but only 17 have been added to the original 10 in the Bill of Rights. One of the weirder ones was renaming the country "United States of Earth."

RAISE THE FLAG

• Since its founding, the U.S. has had 27 versions of its FLAG (a new flag each time new states were added). The current flag was designed by 17-year-old Robert Heft as a school project. He got a B−, but his teacher raised his grade to an A after his flag was chosen by Congress!

• Only four state flags don't contain the color BLUE: Alabama, California, Maryland, and New Mexico.

TRAVELIN'

• The most POPULAR CAR COLOR is white.

• About 5,000 commercial AIRPLANES are flying over the U.S. at any given time.

• The U.S. is the only country to have had astronauts WALK ON THE MOON.

• The LONGEST ROAD (3,365 miles) is U.S.  Route 20 from Boston, Massachusetts, to Newport, Oregon. The MOST-TRAVELED ROAD is Interstate 95 between Florida and Maine. The highest SPEED LIMIT is 85 miles per hour on Texas State Highway 130.

ON THE MAP

• The country's GEOGRAPHIC CENTER (including Alaska and Hawaii) is located near Belle Fourche, South Dakota.

• The FOUR CORNERS MONUMENT is the only point shared by four states: Colorado, Arizona, New Mexico, and Utah.

• The federal government owns 28% of all LAND in the U.S. (including national parks and military facilities). Almost 84% of Nevada and almost 70% of Alaska is government owned.

• The U.S. is the only country with all FIVE CLIMATE ZONES: tropical, dry, temperate, continental, and polar.

• The U.S. claims 14 ISLAND TERRITORIES, including Puerto Rico, Guam, U.S. Virgin Islands, American Samoa, and the Northern Mariana Islands. Did you know Puerto Rico has a larger population than more than 20 states?

ROAD TRIPPIN' U.S.A. BOOKS

• TWO ROADS by Joseph Bruchac

• LOUISIANA'S WAY HOME by Kate DiCamillo

• FROM NORVELT TO NOWHERE by Jack Gantos

• THE REMARKABLE JOURNEY OF COYOTE SUNRISE by Dan Gemeinhart

• THE THING ABOUT LUCK by Cynthia Kadohata

• ROAD TRIP by Gary Paulsen and Jim Paulsen

• CLEAN GETAWAY by Nic Stone

• SISTERS by Raina Telgemeier

SPORTS AND GAMES

• American athletes have won the most OLYMPIC MEDALS. Today, Olympic gold medals are made of silver and only finished with gold.

• The nation's MOST POPULAR SPORT TO WATCH is football.

• The FIRST OFFICIAL INTERNATIONAL MATCH in any sport was a cricket game played between the USA and Canada in 1844 at the St. George's Cricket Club in New York.

• The first known VIDEO GAME competition happened at Stanford University in California in 1972. Players competed in a game called Spacewar. In 1980, the Space Invaders Championship was the first major ESPORTS tournament, with more than 10,000 participants across the U.S.

• The most POPULAR BOARD GAME is chess.

AMERICANS EAT ABOUT: 3 billion pizzas a year (about 46 slices per person)   •   20 billion hot dogs a year (about 70 per person)

THE USA

NAME GAME

- The most popular SURNAME (last name) is Smith.
- Only about 5% of Americans born during the Revolutionary War era had MIDDLE NAMES. By 1900, nearly every American had one.
- The Secret Service uses CODE NAMES for the president, vice president, their families, and prominent officials, such as: Joe Biden—Celtic; Kamala Harris—Pioneer; Donald Trump—Mogul; Mike Pence—Hoosier; Barack Obama—Renegade; Ronald Reagan—Rawhide.

PECULIAR PLACE NAMES

- The nation's most POPULAR CITY NAMES are Franklin, Clinton, Madison, and Washington. The most POPULAR STREET NAMES are Park Street and Second Street.
- Mooselookmeguntic, Maine, and Kleinfeltersville, Pennsylvania, are tied for having the LONGEST TOWN NAMES without spaces or hyphens. The LONGEST STREET NAME is Jean Baptiste Point du Sable Lake Shore Drive.
- What a confusing LOOP OF PLACES! Florida, Ohio › Ohio, Colorado › Colorado, Alaska › Alaska, New Mexico › New Mexico, Maryland › Maryland, New York › New York, Kentucky › Kentucky, Michigan › Michigan, Vermont › Vermont, Indiana › Indiana, Pennsylvania › Pennsylvania, Alabama › Alabama, New York › New York, Texas › Texas, New York › New York, Florida.

SHOW ME THE MONEY

- By law, only DEAD PEOPLE can appear on U.S. currency.
- Paper money was colored green to stop counterfeiting. In the 1800s, cameras only took black and white photographs, making copying GREEN MONEY difficult.
- In 2022, it cost the government 2.72 cents to make a PENNY and 10.41 cents to make a NICKEL.
- The $10,000 BILL used to be the highest denomination in circulation until bills larger than $100 were retired in 1969.

AMAZING ANIMALS

- The BALD EAGLE, the national symbol and national bird, isn't bald—it has white feathers on its head. "Bald" comes from the old English "balde," meaning white. The world's largest known bald eagle nest was discovered in St. Petersburg, Florida. It was 20 feet deep and weighed close to three tons.
- The most POPULAR PETS are dogs and the #1 breed is the French bulldog.
- The most POPULAR PET NAMES are Luna, Max, Bella, Charlie, and Oliver.

2.8 billion pounds of chocolate a year (about 11 pounds per person)

50 billion hamburgers a year (about 154 per person).

Football is a way of life in Alabama. When someone asks "Who are you for?", they're talking about the big rivalry between the University of Alabama ("Roll Tide") and Auburn University ("War Eagle"). But at game-day tailgates, Southern hospitality is on full display with plenty of barbecue, down-home cooking, and sweet tea.

During the Ice Age, GIANT SLOTHS roamed Alabama.

SPACE CAMP at NASA's Marshall Space Flight Center in Huntsville lets you train like an astronaut.

The Yellowhammer State

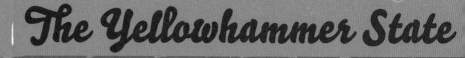

ALABAMA

While in Huntsville, PUT A BANANA ON THE GRAVESTONE of Miss Baker, a squirrel monkey. In 1959, she was the first animal to be launched into space and return safely.

Believe it or NUT, it takes about 810 PEANUTS to make just one jar of peanut butter! Dothan is home to the nation's largest peanut festival.

Alabama has more FAST-FOOD restaurants per person than any other state.

A humongous OFFICE CHAIR, built from 10 tons of steel (that's more than the weight of four cars!), sits in Anniston.

The FIRST PERSON HIT BY A METEORITE was Ann Hodges. In 1954, she was napping on her couch in Sylacauga when a softball-sized meteorite crashed through her ceiling. She survived!

Defy the laws of nature on Gravity Hill in Sylacauga and watch your car appear to ROLL UPHILL BACKWARD!

STATE Favorites

ICE CREAM FLAVOR butter pecan · FRUIT blackberries · COOKIE Yellowhammer cookie

Scottsboro is the LOST LUGGAGE Capital of the World. The huge Unclaimed Baggage Center sells the weird and wonderful contents of suitcases left in airports and train stations.

Every year, in Enterprise, just one person marches in the world's SMALLEST ST. PATRICK'S DAY PARADE!

Don't feed the animals at the ROCK ZOO in Fackler. They're made from painted boulders!

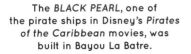

A MAIL BOAT delivers the mail in Magnolia Springs, the only U.S. city with a year-round water delivery route.

The BLACK PEARL, one of the pirate ships in Disney's *Pirates of the Caribbean* movies, was built in Bayou La Batre.

ROSA PARKS is famous for refusing to give up her bus seat to a white person in Montgomery in 1955. Her arrest sparked the Montgomery Bus Boycott and eventually the Civil Rights Act of 1964. But Parks wasn't the first—nine months before, 15-year-old CLAUDETTE COLVIN refused to give up her seat on a Montgomery bus and was also arrested.

In Eufaula, there's a TREE THAT OWNS ITSELF. The oak survived a tornado and a fire in 1919, and in 1936 the town deeded it the land where its roots grow.

The world's largest MOTORCYCLE collection, at the Barber Vintage Motorsports Museum in Birmingham, has over 1,600 motorcycles!

FAST FACTS

CAPITAL Montgomery

FUNNY PLACE NAMES Frog Eye, Gobblers Crossing, Possum Trot, Scratch Ankle, Shinbone Valley, Slicklizzard

STATE SLANG

• Lots of 'Bama kids call their grandparents MEEMAW and PEEPAW.

• A HOT MINUTE means a long-ish amount of time.

The STATE QUARTER features HELEN KELLER reading a book in Braille. The water pump where her teacher spelled the word "water" into her hand is in Tuscumbia.

FANTASTIC FOODS

• ALABAMA WHITE SAUCE is a barbecue favorite made with mayonnaise and lots of black pepper.

• The multilayer LANE CAKE, filled with nuts and dried fruits, was invented by Emma Rylander Lane of Clayton in 1898.

• On New Year's Eve in Mobile, a 12-foot-tall, 350-pound electric MOONPIE is dropped. The MoonPie's a Mardi Gras treat, and Mobile held the first Mardi Gras in the U.S. in 1703.

COOL INVENTIONS

The SUPER SOAKER was invented by Mobile-born Lonnie Johnson. A NASA engineer, Johnson worked on projects such as the Galileo mission to Jupiter by day and created the toy at home at night.

BOOKS *The Watsons Go to Birmingham —1963* by Christopher Paul Curtis • *Gone Crazy in Alabama* by Rita Williams-Garcia

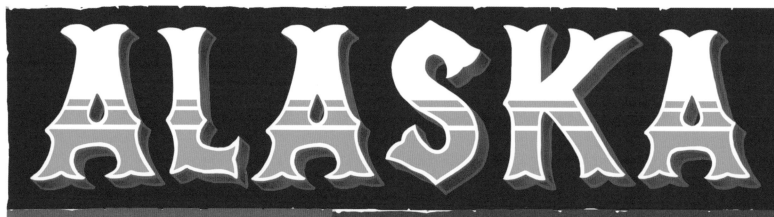

ALASKA

Alaska is a land of opposites. It's the largest state in area, but has the fewest people per square mile. It has the most coastlines, glaciers, and lakes, yet the fewest roads. And it has the longest summer days and the longest winter nights. With snowy mountains, immense icebergs, dense forests, and wonderful wild animals, there's never a dull moment in exciting Alaska!

The Last Frontier

Alaska is home to about 17 trillion MOSQUITOES. Their combined weight is about 96 million pounds!

Alaska is the only state name that can be typed on ONE ROW of a keyboard.

The STATE FLAG was designed in 1927 by 13-year-old Benny Benson, who won a contest.

Ketchikan has the highest ZIP CODE in the U.S. (99950). It also has the world's largest collection of TOTEM POLES.

Alaska has the nation's BIGGEST INDIGENOUS POPULATION, with 229 tribal nations and 20 Indigenous languages spoken.

Fairbanks is the best place to see the AURORA BOREALIS (Northern Lights)—the display is visible about 243 days a year.

A man in Cooper Landing has one of the world's largest collections of FOUR-LEAF CLOVERS. By 2007, he'd found 111,060. The chance of finding a four-leaf clover is 1 in 10,000!

The IDITAROD TRAIL SLED DOG RACE is Alaska's largest sporting event. The dogs all wear waterproof booties to protect their paws from ice, snow, and rocks.

The town of North Pole has the world's largest SANTA CLAUS statue (42 feet high!).

State Favorites

BREAKFAST reindeer sausage · SNACK smoked salmon jerky · FRUIT wild blueberries

Land of the Midnight Sun

Prospect Creek holds the record for the nation's **LOWEST TEMPERATURE**, hitting −80 degrees Fahrenheit on January 23rd, 1971.

At the **OUTHOUSE RACES** at the Fur Rendezvous Festival in Anchorage, teams strap skis onto homemade outhouses and push or pull them (with one person sitting on the potty!) to the finish line.

The **MIDNIGHT SUN BASEBALL GAME** is played at midnight on the summer solstice (the longest day of the year). On this day, the sun shines for 24 hours in Fairbanks.

For 20 years, Talkeetna's elected **MAYOR** was a **CAT** named Stubbs (he didn't have a tail).

The **MOST POWERFUL EARTHQUAKE** in U.S. history (9.2 on the Richter scale) shook Prince William Sound in 1964.

By law, only Alaskan residents are allowed to **DIP NET**. In this popular sport, fish are scooped out of a river with a huge, long-handled net.

Alaskan farmers grow some of the largest **VEGGIES** in the world, including a 138-pound cabbage and a 2,051-pound pumpkin!

FAST FACTS

CAPITAL Juneau

FUNNY PLACE NAMES
Chicken, Deadhorse, Funny River, Unalaska (yep, Unalaska, Alaska)

STATE SLANG
• A **SOURDOUGH** is someone who's made it through an Alaskan winter. Legend has it early miners slept curled around their sourdough starter (yeast) in winter to keep it warm enough to bake fresh bread.

• A **CHEECHAKO** is a newcomer to Alaska.

The **STATE QUARTER** features a **GRIZZLY BEAR** with a **SALMON** in its mouth. The largest salmon ever caught (97 pounds, 4 ounces) was at the Kenai River.

FANTASTIC FOODS
• Inuit families enjoy **AGUTUK** or **ALASKAN ICE CREAM**, traditionally made from seal oil, reindeer fat, snow, and berries.

• Jumbo **RED KING CRAB** legs are served with garlic butter and a squirt of lemon.

COOL INVENTIONS
• Native Alaskans have been slicing and dicing with the **ULU KNIFE** since 2500 BCE.

• In 1949, a plumber working out in the bush (the rural area of the state) invented the first **RANCH DRESSING** to get his crew to eat the salad he'd made. He later sold it as Hidden Valley Ranch.

BOOKS *Balto and the Great Race* by Elizabeth Cody Kimmel • *Chia and the Fox Man* adapted by Barbara J. Atwater and Ethan J. Atwater

With its wavy red rock walls and narrow passageways, Antelope Canyon in Page is the most-visited SLOT CANYON in the Southwest.

A meteorite slammed into Earth about 50,000 years ago, leaving the $\frac{3}{4}$-mile -wide Barringer METEOR CRATER in Winslow.

ARIZONA

The Grand Canyon State

Oatman, a ghost town where WILD BURROS roam the streets, gets so hot that it hosts a SIDEWALK EGG FRY CHALLENGE every July 4th!

Slip on your sunglasses and hop in the pool, 'cause it's hot, hot, hot in Arizona! The state boasts triple-digit temperatures, less than 13 inches of rain a year, and well over 200 days of bright sunshine. In fact, Arizona is one of only two states (the other's Hawaii) that don't take part in daylight saving time. Why not? They don't need extra hours of sun during the day! Home to the famous Grand Canyon, this Wild West state has incredible deserts, red sandstone cliffs, cacti, and cloud-free skies.

From a BAT TUNNEL in Phoenix, around 10,000 Mexican free-tailed bats take flight at dusk and swarm the sky.

Do you think hula-hooping is hard? Try hoop dancing! Native dancers wearing specially made colorful regalia twirl up to 50 handmade hoops at one time! The World Championship HOOP DANCE COMPETITION is held each year in Phoenix.

Yuma is the SUNNIEST place in the world.

NAVAJO (Diné) is the most widely spoken language in Arizona after English and Spanish.

The GILA MONSTER, the only venomous lizard native to the U.S., lives in Arizona.

STaTe Favorites

COOKIE Mexican wedding cookie • DESSERT sopaipillas • BREAKFAST chilaquiles

FAST FACTS

CAPITAL Phoenix

FUNNY PLACE NAMES Bumble Bee, Christmas, Happy Jack, Show Low, Skull Valley, Surprise, Why

STATE SLANG

• A **HABOOB** is a massive desert dust storm. The dust can form a wall over a mile high and 100 miles wide!

• A **CHUBASCO** is a violent summer rain with lightning and thunder.

The **STATE QUARTER** features the **GRAND CANYON** and a **SAGUARO** cactus. One of the Seven Natural Wonders of the World, the Grand Canyon is a mile-deep gorge sculpted by the mighty Colorado River. Locals call it "The Big Ditch."

FANTASTIC FOODS

• The **SONORAN DOG,** a bacon-wrapped hot dog covered in beans, chopped tomatoes, mayo, onions, and jalapeño sauce, is a popular street food.

• The bright purple fruit of the **PRICKLY PEAR CACTUS** tastes like a mix of watermelon and bubblegum.

COOL INVENTIONS

• When Clayton Jacobson II wanted a "motorcycle for the water," he invented the **JET SKI** in the 1960s.

• The **BOLO TIE** is the official state necktie. Victor Emanuel Cedarstaff of Wickenburg is credited with inventing it in the late 1940s.

BOOKS *Stargirl* by Jerry Spinelli • *Weedflower* by Cynthia Kadohata

Old LONDON BRIDGE in England was falling down (just like the nursery rhyme says). Robert P. McCulloch purchased it and had it shipped to Lake Havasu City, where it was rebuilt brick by brick in 1968.

Famous for the legendary gunfight at the O.K. Corral, the Old West town of TOMBSTONE has a graveyard called "Boot Hill." Outlaws who "died with their boots on" are buried here.

The SAGUARO is the largest cactus in the U.S., growing to 40 feet tall (that's like a giraffe standing on top of another giraffe!). It's against state law to dig up and move a saguaro cactus.

There's a FOREST MADE OF STONE! The Petrified Forest National Park is packed with fossilized logs dating back 225 million years.

The LAVA RIVER CAVE near Flagstaff is a mile-long tube of once-molten rock and is more than 700,000 years old.

Arizona has 13 species of RATTLESNAKE, more than in any other state. A group of rattlesnakes is called a rhumba!

The OSTRICH Festival in Chandler celebrates ostrich ranching, which was popular here in the early 1900s.

Some folks find saying this state name tricky. The correct pronunciation is AR-ken-saw (please, please don't upset the locals by mispronouncing it AR-Kansas). Arkansas is nicknamed the "Natural State" because not only does it have the Ozark and Ouachita Mountains, 2.5 million acres of national forest, 52 state parks, rivers, and lakes; but also hot springs, bayous, swamps, and diamonds!

Crater of Diamonds State Park near Murfreesboro is the only active DIAMOND MINE in the nation. Visitors can take home any diamond they dig up! In 1990, Shirley Strawn hit the jackpot when she unearthed the first-ever perfect diamond. Did you know the chance of finding a flawless diamond is one in a billion?

The first FRIED DILL PICKLE was sold in Atkins in 1963. Every May, the town holds a Picklefest with a pickle juice drinking contest.

ARKANSAS
The Natural State

Mountain View is the FOLK MUSIC capital of the world and one of the world's largest producers of handmade DULCIMERS.

At the World's Championship DUCK CALLING Contest in Stuttgart, contestants blow into a small whistle to mimic different calls, or sounds, ducks make.

The World CHEESE DIP Championship is held in Little Rock. Cheese dip was said to be first made in Arkansas in 1935.

The official state beverage is MILK.

It's said that OLD NAKED JOE MOUNTAIN in the Ozarks is named after a man who used to run about without his clothes!

In Pine Bluff, Ben Pearson was the first in the country to mass-produce BOWS and ARROWS.

A huge water tower is painted to look like a spinach can in Alma, the SPINACH Capital of the World (the title's also claimed by Crystal Springs, Texas).

State Favorites   SANDWICH fried bologna · FRUIT grapes · HALLOWEEN CANDY Jolly Ranchers

Legend has it the seven-foot-tall, hairy BOGGY CREEK MONSTER, a Southern version of Bigfoot, has been spotted near Fouke.

The PINK TOMATO is both the state fruit AND the state vegetable, because technically it's a fruit, but it's eaten like a vegetable. Take a juicy bite at the tomato-eating contest at the Bradley County Pink Tomato Festival.

It's against state law for a PINBALL MACHINE to give away more than 25 free games to a player who keeps winning.

TEXARKANA

TEXAS | STATE LINE | ARKANSAS

Nine Black students, called THE LITTLE ROCK NINE, helped advance the desegregation of public schools in the South when they courageously volunteered to attend all-white Little Rock Central High School in 1957.

The community of TEXARKANA is in both Arkansas and Texas. There are two different city governments—and a line divides the shared post office and the courthouse in half.

The Basin Park Hotel in Eureka Springs is seven stories tall, yet EVERY FLOOR IS THE "GROUND FLOOR" because the hotel is built against the side of a mountain.

FAST FACTS

CAPITAL Little Rock

FUNNY PLACE NAMES Accident, Booger Hollow, Fifty-Six, Forty-Four, Greasy Corner, Monkey Run, Okay, Possum Grape, Toad Suck

STATE SLANG
- Someone who's MADDER THAN A WET HEN is very, very angry.
- Something CATTYWAMPUS is askew or wonky.

The **STATE QUARTER** features RICE STALKS, a DIAMOND, and a MALLARD DUCK flying over a lake. Arkansas is the #1 producer of rice in the U.S.

FANTASTIC FOODS
- Chocolate rules! Biscuits with CHOCOLATE GRAVY are a breakfast tradition. A CHOCOLATE ROLL is a long, buttery pastry filled with chocolate, and Searcy County is the Chocolate Roll Capital of the World.
- CHEESE DOGS (cheese inside a hot dog) were created in Little Rock in 1956.

COOL INVENTIONS
- Sam Walton started a small five-and-dime store in Rogers in 1962 that grew to become the superstore chain WALMART. You can visit the Walmart Museum in Bentonville.

BOOKS *March Forward, Girl: From Young Warrior to Little Rock Nine* by Melba Pattillo Beals • *Making Friends with Billy Wong* by Augusta Scattergood

When people talk about this enormous state with the biggest population in the U.S. (home to one in eight Americans), they tend to divide it in two: Northern and Southern. NorCal has the chill vibes of San Francisco, the tech hub of Silicon Valley, the vineyards of Napa Valley, gold rush cities, and towering redwood forests. SoCal has the glam and glitz of Los Angeles and Hollywood, sunny beaches and surf culture, vast deserts, and Disneyland. Put both halves together, and there's nothing you can't do in California!

The Golden State

Steer your car through the trunk of an ancient, giant redwood at the CHANDELIER DRIVE-THRU TREE in Leggett. The tree's name comes from its enormous branches, which hang 100 feet above the ground like a chandelier.

Go HIGH or go LOW? Mount Whitney, the highest point in the contiguous U.S., is only 76 miles from Death Valley, the lowest point in North America.

Death Valley is the HOTTEST PLACE ON EARTH. On July 10th, 1913, it reached 134 degrees Fahrenheit—the highest temperature ever recorded.

The small mountain town of Willow Creek is the BIGFOOT Capital of the World. Hundreds of curious people come to search for the mythic large, hairy beast.

Try GARLIC ICE CREAM at the Gilroy Garlic Festival!

HAMBURGERS

Yosemite Falls is one of the HIGHEST WATERFALLS in North America.

Brothers Dick and Mac McDonald opened their first HAMBURGER restaurant in San Bernardino in 1948.

Get loud at the COYOTE HOWL contest in Coulterville.

It's against state law to eat a FROG if it dies in a frog-jumping contest.

Hop on over to the BUNNY Museum in Altadena to see over 40,000 bunny items on display, including bunny-shaped bushes.

Good luck trying an "around the world" with the enormous 256-pound wooden YO-YO at Chico's National Yo-Yo Museum.

State Favorites

DOUGHNUT bear claw · SANDWICH French dip · BREAKFAST avocado toast

CALIFORNIA

Don't lean on the walls in BUBBLEGUM ALLEY in San Luis Obispo! They're covered with over 2 million pieces of chewed gum left by people who've walked by.

The bright-yellow International BANANA Museum in Mecca has the world's largest collection of banana-related items.

At the Pageant of the Masters in Laguna Beach, real people pose to recreate famous artwork or "LIVING PICTURES" on stage.

Venice, California, has CANALS—just like Venice, Italy.

There are more CARS in Los Angeles than people.

TOP CROPS! California produces almost all of the country's almonds, apricots, avocados, artichokes, carrots, cauliflower, celery, dates, figs, garlic, grapes, lemons, lettuce, kiwis, nectarines, olives, plums, pomegranates, strawberries, and walnuts.

FAST FACTS

CAPITAL Sacramento

FUNNY PLACE NAMES Badwater, Cool, Doghouse Junction, Fallen Leaf, Nice, Rough and Ready, Teakettle Junction, You Bet, Zzyzx

STATE SLANG
• "That BREAK was GNARLY," is surfer-speak for "the waves were really good but challenging."

• "Let's CRUISE OVER to IN-N-OUT," means "let's take a drive to In-N-Out Burger," the iconic burger chain founded in California in 1948.

The STATE QUARTER features naturalist JOHN MUIR admiring YOSEMITE National Park. A CALIFORNIA CONDOR, the largest flying bird in North America, soars in the sky.

FANTASTIC FOODS
• SRIRACHA hot sauce is made in Rosemead. There's a rooster on the bottle, because the company's founder was born in the Chinese year of the rooster.

• CIOPPINO is a hearty fish stew from San Francisco.

• The FORTUNE COOKIE was created at the Golden Gate Park Japanese Tea Garden in San Francisco around 1900.

COOL INVENTIONS
• POPSICLES were invented when a San Francisco teenager accidentally left a sweet drink outside in the cold in 1905!

• SKATEBOARDS started as a way for surfers to practice their skills on land.

• The plastic HULA-HOOP was invented in a family garage in Pasadena in 1958. Arthur "Spud" Melin and Richard Kneer got the idea from Australian children's bamboo exercise rings.

BOOKS *Esperanza Rising* by Pam Muñoz Ryan • *Front Desk* by Kelly Yang

Have some EIGHT-LEGGED FUN at the Tarantula Festival in Coarsegold with a live tarantula derby and hairy leg contest (for humans)!

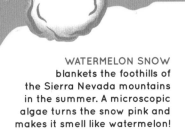

WATERMELON SNOW blankets the foothills of the Sierra Nevada mountains in the summer. A microscopic algae turns the snow pink and makes it smell like watermelon!

Colorado's natural beauty is off the charts! It even inspired Katharine Lee Bates to write the famous song "America the Beautiful" in 1895. Standing on top of Pike's Peak, she spied "amber waves of grain," where today cattle graze the rolling plains. She took in "purple mountain majesties" where skiers and snowboarders now zoom down the snowcapped Rockies. She may also have spotted Great Sand Dune National Park, where sand boarders now "shred" the tallest sand dunes in North America.

Grand Mesa is the largest FLAT-TOP MOUNTAIN in the world.

The BIGGEST SNOWFALL over a 24-hour period in the U.S. measured 75.8 inches in Silver Lake in 1921. A tall adult standing up would've been completely buried in snow that day.

COLORADO

The Centennial State

In 1894, the largest SILVER NUGGET ever (1,840 pounds) was dug up in Aspen. Mined silver is purified then melted before being poured into molds to form bars.

In Glenwood Springs, the world's largest NATURAL HOT SPRINGS POOL has over 1 million gallons of steaming water.

MIKE THE HEADLESS CHICKEN Festival in Fruita honors the spirit of a chicken that had its head cut off in 1945—yet lived until 1947!

The nation's largest FORK is in Creede. It's 40 feet long and weighs over 600 pounds.

SILVER

It's believed RODEO started in 1869 in Deer Trail, when cowboys from nearby ranches competed to see who was better at breaking wild horses.

The Royal Gorge Bridge is the HIGHEST SUSPENSION BRIDGE in the U.S. It's perched 955 feet over the Arkansas River.

Use your hands, a catapult, or even a cannon to hurl a fruitcake at the GREAT FRUITCAKE TOSS in Manitou Springs!

State Favorites ICE CREAM FLAVOR rocky road · JELLY BEAN FLAVOR licorice · PIZZA TOPPING basil

Watch SKI JORING races in Leadville. In ski joring, a skier holds onto a rope and is pulled by a galloping horse (with a rider) through a snow-packed course with jumps, gates, and rings.

The UFO WATCHTOWER outside of Hooper offers prime viewing for extraterrestrial activity. The San Luis Valley is often called "The Bermuda Triangle of the West" due to all the otherworldly sightings.

Colfax Avenue in Denver is the LONGEST CONTINUOUS STREET in the U.S.

A 15-foot-tall TROLL sculpture in Breckenridge, named Isak Heartstone, has a heart-shaped stone hidden inside its body.

At the annual Emma Crawford COFFIN RACES in Manitou Springs, teams push decorated coffins (with an "Emma" inside) to the finish line. In 1891, Emma was buried at the top of the highest peak, and her coffin slid down the mountainside during a rainstorm 38 years later.

Go for a spin at the Lee Maxwell WASHING MACHINE Museum in Eaton.

It's against Colorado law to pick the state flower, the COLUMBINE, on public land.

Denver is called THE MILE-HIGH CITY. The 13th step of the state capital building is exactly one mile above sea level.

FAST FACTS

CAPITAL Denver

FUNNY PLACE NAMES Crook, Dinosaur, Fairplay, Hygiene, Kinikinik (spelled the same forward and backward!), Last Chance, No Name, Tin Cup

STATE SLANG
- "Let's **HIT THE HILL** and ride our **LUNCH TRAYS** 'cause the **POW-POW** is **SICK**," means: "Let's go to the slopes and ride our snowboards, because the fresh, powdery snow is amazing."

- When someone brags about climbing a **14-ER**, they're talking about mountains over 14,000 feet high. Colorado has 58—more than any other state.

The **STATE QUARTER** features the majestic **ROCKY MOUNTAINS**. Colorado is the "Centennial State," because it became a state on the 100th birthday of the United States.

FANTASTIC FOODS
- **GREEN CHILE** is a green sauce made from stewed Hatch green chiles.

- The **DENVER OMELET**, also called Western omelet, is made with ham, onion, and bell pepper.

- The first **ROOT BEER FLOAT** (vanilla ice cream in root beer) was made by Frank J. Wisner of Cripple Creek in 1893. He originally called it the "Black Cow."

COOL INVENTIONS
- Denver-born Ruth Handler invented the **BARBIE DOLL** in 1959.

- The hard candy **JOLLY RANCHER** was invented in 1949 by Bill Harmsen from Golden. The first three flavors were apple, grape, and "fire stix."

BOOKS *Prairie School* by Avi • *The Girl Who Thought in Pictures: The Story of Dr. Temple Grandin* by Julia Finley Mosca

Connecticut got its "Constitution State" nickname because the laws and rules in The Fundamental Orders of Connecticut (1639) were used as a blueprint for the U.S. CONSTITUTION.

The Lock Museum of America in Terryville has the largest collection of antique LOCKS in the U.S.

The Constitution State

CONNECTICUT

In 1900, Louis Lassen put ground beef between slices of toast and made what's claimed to be the first HAMBURGER. It's still served at his New Haven restaurant, Louis' Lunch, but there's one rule: no ketchup allowed. Ever.

It's fitting that the country's first cookbook was published in Connecticut in 1796, because this small state (third smallest in the nation) has a big appetite when it comes to food. It's the home of the steamed cheeseburger, clambakes, shad bakes (the state fish), clam pizza, hot lobster rolls, the Almond Joy and Mounds bars, Milano cookies and Goldfish crackers, and the first Subway sandwiches. Yum!

It's against state rules to call or label a PICKLE a "pickle" unless it bounces.

Every Friday, volunteers known as "Old Cranks" hand-wind hundreds of timepieces on display at the American CLOCK and WATCH Museum in Bristol (once the country's clock-making capital).

Don't throw stones when you visit architect Philip Johnson's GLASS HOUSE in New Canaan!

The PEZ factory's Visitor Center in Orange has the largest public collection of PEZ memorabilia. The company's name comes from "pfefferminz," the German word for "peppermint."

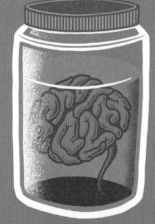

Over 400 BRAINS FLOATING IN JARS can be found at the Cushing Brain Collection in the basement of Yale University's Medical Library.

STate Favorites

HALLOWEEN CANDY Almond Joy · PIZZA TOPPING Clams · COOKIE Snickerdoodle

FAST FACTS

CAPITAL Hartford

FUNNY PLACE NAMES Cos Cob, Happyland, Hazardville, Mystic, Terramuggus, Woodtick

STATE SLANG

• APIZZA (pronounced "ah-beetz") is thin-crust pizza found in and around New Haven.

• A TAG SALE is a garage sale.

• The STATE QUARTER features the CHARTER OAK TREE. In 1687, the charter (a legal document giving Connecticut self-rule) was hidden inside the tree to keep it safe from the British.

FANTASTIC FOODS

• A GRINDER is a submarine-style sandwich with meat, cheese, and fixings on a roll.

• The first LOBSTER ROLL was served in 1929 in Milford. Connecticut lobster rolls are served hot with melted butter.

COOL INVENTIONS

• The first modern LOLLIPOP was invented in New Haven in 1908 by George Smith, who named the candy on a stick after a popular racehorse, Lolly Pop.

• The FRISBEE got its name by accident. The Frisbie Pie Company in Bridgeport sold their pies to nearby universities. The students would throw and catch the empty pie tins, calling out "Frisbie!"

• Edwin H. Land from Bridgeport invented the first instant camera, the POLAROID Land Camera, in 1948.

BOOKS *Because of Mr. Terupt* by Rob Buyea • *The Baby-Sitters Club* series by Ann M. Martin

The Scoville Memorial Library (1771) in Salisbury was the country's first PUBLIC LIBRARY open free of charge.

Hundreds of fossilized three-toed DINOSAUR PRINTS were discovered at Dinosaur State Park in Rocky Hill.

The Barnum Museum in Bridgeport celebrates the life of P.T. BARNUM, founder of the Barnum & Bailey Circus.

The Frog Bridge in Willimantic is decorated with GIANT FROGS sitting on spools of thread.

Residents of Newington claim Mill Pond Falls is the nation's SMALLEST NATURAL WATERFALL.

Since 1771, voters in Hartford have been eating nutmeg-spiced ELECTION CAKE to celebrate voting on Election Day.

The University of Connecticut is the only U.S. university to offer undergraduate and graduate degrees in PUPPETRY.

The funny-looking STAR-NOSED MOLE is found underground in wetlands throughout Connecticut.

The Nutmeg State

The First State

Delaware Bay has the world's largest population of HORSESHOE CRABS. Horseshoe crabs can go a year without eating and have been around since the age of the dinosaurs.

RETURN DAY is held the Thursday after an election in Georgetown. The winners and losers literally bury a hatchet in a sandbox to show there are no hard feelings.

CHICKENS outnumber people 200-to-1 in Delaware (the chicken population is over 200 million!).

Legend has it that PEA PATCH ISLAND got its name when a ship carrying peas ran aground and the crew dumped them to lighten the load. The peas sprouted new plants all over the island.

A second-grade class convinced Delaware to choose the LADYBUG as the official state bug. Many cultures believe ladybugs bring good luck.

FAST FACTS

CAPITAL Dover

FUNNY PLACE NAMES Bear, Blackbird, Cabbage Corner, Flea Hill, Hourglass, Long Neck, Mermaid, Pepperbox, Red Lion, Shortly

STATE SLANG
If someone's _____, they're laughing uncontrollably.

The _____ is the southern half of the state, which is more rural and relaxed.

The **STATE QUARTER** features _____, one of Delaware's delegates to the 2nd Continental Congress. On July 1st, 1776, he raced 18 hours to Philadelphia, despite severe thunderstorms and suffering from cancer, to cast the deciding vote in favor of signing the Declaration of Independence.

FANTASTIC FOODS
_____ are flat, square noodles served in a rich gravy with baked chicken.

_____ is a Thanksgiving-inspired sandwich packed with roast turkey, stuffing, and cranberry sauce.

Popular for breakfast, _____ is made from pork scraps formed into a loaf. Enjoy some at the Apple-Scrapple Festival in Bridgeville!

COOL INVENTIONS
_____, the first synthetic fiber, was invented in the 1930s by chemist Dr. Wallace Carothers at the DuPont research laboratories in Seaford. Among many other things, it's used in swimsuits, guitar strings, parachutes, umbrellas, and sleeping bags.

Until the late 1920s, Americans didn't eat much chicken. Small family farms raised them mostly for eggs. In 1923, Cecile Steele of Ocean View ordered 50 chicks, but the company accidentally sent her 500! She decided to raise them as "meat birds," not egg-layers. Five years later, she had around 25,000 chickens and had started the _____. Chicken is now the country's most-eaten meat.

BOOKS *A Light in the Storm (Dear America)* by Karen Hesse   *We Dream of Space* by Erin Entrada Kelly

In 2022, 72-year-old Lynnea C. Salvo became the oldest woman to CROSS AMERICA BY BICYCLE. She peddled from the US-Canada border to California in just 43 days.

The first LOG CABINS in America were built in the 1600s by Swedish settlers near the Delaware River.

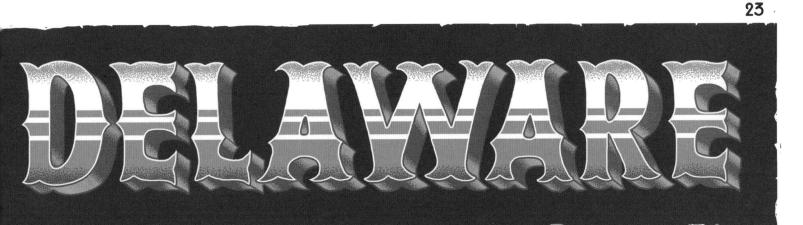

DELAWARE

Delaware (the second-smallest state) is known as the "First State," because it was the first to ratify the U.S. Constitution, but it also has another nickname—the "Diamond State." As the story goes, Thomas Jefferson called Delaware a "jewel" because of its superior location. Wedged between New Jersey, Pennsylvania, and Maryland, and only 35 miles across at its widest point, tiny Delaware links the Southeast to the Northeast.

THE DIAMOND STATE

Sit inside a GIANT BIRD'S NEST at Winterthur Museum and Gardens in Wilmington.

The Great Delaware Kite Festival began in 1969, when the Maharajah of Bharatpur, India, challenged the Governor of Delaware to a KITE-FLYING DUEL. To win, one flyer's kite string had to cut the other's in air.

Inhale the scent of thousands of fragrant purple flowers at LAVENDER Fields Farm in Milton.

MUSKRAT (a rodent found by rivers and marshes) was once a Delaware dinner tradition. Southern Grille in Ellendale still offers it on their menu. It's your choice: do you want your muskrat served head-on or head-off?

BRRRRR! Every February, thousands of swimmers dive into the frigid waters of the Atlantic Ocean at the annual Lewes POLAR BEAR PLUNGE at Rehoboth Beach.

Bring your broom to compete in the BROOM-TOSSING CONTEST at the Sea Witch Festival in Rehoboth.

The Cannonball House in Lewes still has a CANNONBALL shot by the British during the War of 1812 embedded in it.

State Favorites **ICE CREAM FLAVOR** cookie dough • **DESSERT** peach pie • **SNACK** crab dip with Ritz crackers

FLORIDA

THE SUNSHINE STATE

The Florida MANATEE Festival in Crystal River is a celebration of all things sea cow.

St. Joseph calls itself the KUMQUAT Capital of the World. Kumquats are a small orange-yellow fruit with a tangy taste.

The 10-day American SANDSCULPTING Championship on Fort Myers Beach is like the Olympics of sand sculptures.

The nation's SMALLEST POST OFFICE in Ochopee is only 61.3 square feet.

With more than 400 species of shell, Sanibel Island has the best beaches for finding SEA SHELLS.

3...2...1... blast off! Brevard County's area code 321 honors the rocket countdown at NASA'S KENNEDY SPACE CENTER (launch site for every U.S. crewed space flight since 1968).

The SKUNK APE—a huge, hairy, smelly beast said to roam the Everglades wetlands—is Florida's version of Bigfoot.

The Everglades is the only place in the world where both ALLIGATORS and CROCODILES live.

The CORAL CASTLE Museum in Miami, carved out of over 1,100 tons of coral rock, has a nine-ton gate that can be opened with just one finger!

At the WORM GRUNTIN' Festival in Sopchoppy, people charm worms out of the ground by rubbing pieces of wood and metal together. The vibrations trick the worms into thinking a mole is coming to eat them, so they slither to the surface, where they're scooped for fish bait.

Florida has more GOLF COURSES than any other state.

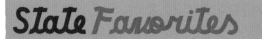

State Favorites

JUICE orange · ICE CREAM FLAVOR cookie dough · PIZZA TOPPING pineapple

Abundant sunshine makes Florida the perfect state for growing juicy citrus, such as oranges, grapefruits, and tangerines. It also makes for fabulous beach days, because no matter where you are, you're never more than an hour and a half from the ocean. Why's that? Florida's a peninsula, surrounded by water on three sides. In fact, only Alaska has more coastline than Florida.

FAST FACTS

CAPITAL Tallahassee

FUNNY PLACE NAMES
Celebration, Christmas, Dogtown, Early Bird, Fluffy Landing, Frostproof, Spuds, Treasure Island, Two Egg, Utopia

STATE SLANG
• **NO-SEE-UMS** are annoying, teeny-tiny, biting bugs.

• If the rain's a **TOAD-STRANGLER**, it means it's really coming down. In Miami, a huge storm is called a **PALMETTO POUNDER**.

The **STATE QUARTER** features a 16th-century **GALLEON** ship (sailed by the first Spanish explorers), a **SPACE SHUTTLE** (flown by U.S. astronauts to explore outer space), and **PALMETTO** palm trees (the state tree).

FLORIDA 1845 — GATEWAY TO DISCOVERY

FANTASTIC FOODS
• True **KEY LIME PIE,** the tart-and-sweet pie created in Key West, is yellow and not green. The Florida Keys are islands. "Key" comes from the Spanish word "cayo," meaning "small island."

• The **CUBANO** is a pressed sandwich with ham, mojo roast pork, pickles, mustard, and Swiss cheese on thick Cuban bread. Florida has the most Cuban-Americans of any state.

• **STONE CRABS** are a Florida delicacy served cold with a tangy mustard dipping sauce.

COOL INVENTIONS
• Benjamin Green, a Miami pharmacist, invented **SUNSCREEN.** During World War II, he protected himself from ultraviolet rays with thick, greasy "red vet pet" (red veterinary petrolatum). After the war, he mixed red vet pet, cocoa butter, and coconut oil, and this became Coppertone suntan lotion.

BOOKS *Because of Winn-Dixie* by Kate DiCamillo
• *Merci Suárez Changes Gears* by Meg Medina

Find ancient SHARK TEETH buried in the sand at Venice, the "Shark Tooth Capital of the World."

A huge network of SECRET TUNNELS under WALT DISNEY WORLD, the most-visited theme park in the world, lets "cast members," or employees, quickly get from one end to the other.

Aquarius Reef Base—the world's only UNDERSEA RESEARCH LAB—sits on the ocean floor, 62 feet below sea level off the coast of Key Largo.

There's supposedly over a trillion dollars of LOST TREASURE waiting to be found off the Florida coast!

Jam out at the Lower Keys UNDERWATER MUSIC FESTIVAL, an undersea concert for scuba divers and snorkelers.

It's against state law to have public DOORS open inward. (It's easier to escape hurricanes this way.)

Fellsmere's FROG LEG Festival holds the record for most frog legs served in one day!

There's lots of delicious eating to be done in Georgia! Take a big bite from the world's largest peach cobbler at the Georgia Peach Festival (it's the "Peach State," after all). Then visit Albany—the pecan capital of the U.S. with more than 600,000 pecan trees—for a slice of gooey pecan pie. After that, grab a handful of boiled, warm goobers (also known as peanuts) and see how many onions you can gulp down in the Vidalia Onion Eating Contest. (Yep, Georgia also produces the most peanuts and sweet Vidalia onions!)

WESLEYAN COLLEGE in Macon was the first U.S. college chartered to grant women college degrees.

Swim with whale sharks and shake hands with otters at the Georgia Aquarium, the largest AQUARIUM in the U.S., with more than 100,000 aquatic animals in over 10 million gallons of water.

Civil rights leader MARTIN LUTHER KING, JR. gave his first public speech at age 15 at First African Baptist Church in Dublin.

Get buggy at the FIRE ANT Festival in Ashburn. Or check out the over 1 million blood-sucking TICKS on display at the U.S. National Tick Collection at Georgia Southern University.

Atlanta is a hub of HIP-HOP and RAP, with more than a dozen top labels producing chart-topping music.

STUCKIE THE MUMMIFIED DOG is "stuck" at Southern Forest World in Waycross. While hunting in the 1960s, Stuckie chased an animal into a hollow tree, got stuck, died —and became a dog mummy!

Approximately 90% of the world's CARPET comes from Dalton, the "Carpet Capital of the World."

Screaming Eagle at Banning Mills is one of the world's longest and largest ZIPLINE canopy tours. Zip through the air at 70 miles per hour!

Hartsfield–Jackson Atlanta International Airport is the world's BUSIEST AIRPORT in number of passengers served.

Atlanta LIGHTS UP THE NIGHT with dazzling events such as the Chinese Lantern Festival and the BeltLine Lantern Parade.

CDC, the Centers for DISEASE CONTROL AND PREVENTION in Atlanta, aims to prevent the spread of illness and disease throughout the nation. It's also one of only two labs in the world allowed to store vials of the variola (smallpox) virus.

State Favorites   PIZZA TOPPING mushrooms · SNACK fried green tomatoes · HALLOWEEN CANDY Swedish Fish

GEORGIA

The Peach State

VARSITY

The Varsity in Atlanta is the world's largest DRIVE-IN fast-food restaurant, taking up two city blocks and serving their famous chili dogs.

It's against state law to eat FRIED CHICKEN with anything but your fingers in Gainesville—no knife or fork!

The Okefenokee is the largest SWAMP in North America. Carnivorous (meat-eating) pitcher plants grow here. Some are so large they can eat a frog!

Cumberland Island is inhabited by WILD HORSES.

Old Car City in White is the world's largest CAR JUNKYARD, with more than 4,000 classic cars.

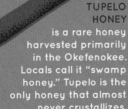

An Alpharetta dentist owns the world's largest collection of TOOTHPASTE. Wacky flavors such as spicy wasabi, eggplant, and pumpkin pudding are among his over 3,000 tubes.

TUPELO HONEY is a rare honey harvested primarily in the Okefenokee. Locals call it "swamp honey." Tupelo is the only honey that almost never crystallizes.

FAST FACTS

CAPITAL Atlanta

FUNNY PLACE NAMES Between, Butts, Cloudland, Coffee, Enigma, Experiment, Hopeulikit, Santa Claus, Shake Rag, Thunderbolt, Tiger

STATE SLANG
• **"GET TO GETTIN', Y'ALL!"** means it's time for everyone to leave.

• **"QUIT BEING UGLY,"** means "stop being so mean," or "stop gossiping."

The STATE QUARTER features a **PEACH** (the state fruit) and branches from a **LIVE OAK** (the state tree).

FANTASTIC FOODS
• **PIMENTO CHEESE** is a Southern classic, combining sharp cheddar cheese, mayo, and tangy red pimento peppers into a spread or dip.

• **COCA-COLA CAKE** is a chocolate sheet cake that has a cup of cola in the batter.

COOL INVENTIONS
• **COCA-COLA** was invented in 1886 by Atlanta pharmacist John Pemberton. At the World of Coca-Cola museum, you can sample beverages from around the world.

• In 1955, two neighbors in Avondale Estates found themselves hungry at night, so they opened a 24-hour restaurant they named **WAFFLE HOUSE**. That first restaurant is now the Waffle House Museum.

BOOKS *Ida Early Comes Over the Mountain* by Robert Burch • *Kira-Kira* by Cynthia Kadohata

HAWAII

THE ALOHA STATE

Hawaii—spelled Hawai'i in the Hawaiian language—is made up of 137 tropical islands in the Pacific Ocean. There are eight major islands, each with an official color: Oahu (yellow); Maui (pink); Hawaii Island, also known as the Big Island (red); Kauai (purple); Lanai (orange); Molokai (green); Niihau (white); and Kahoolawe (gray). Hawaii's many beaches bring the rainbow too—you'll find white, yellow, black, red, and even green sand!

The PINEAPPLE Garden Maze at Dole Plantation is the world's largest plant maze. Find your way through the 2.5-mile labyrinth in record time to win a prize!

Iolani Palace in Honolulu, built in 1882 by King Kalakaua, is the only ROYAL PALACE in the U.S.

The three-day HULA COMPETITION at the Merrie Monarch Festival in Hilo is sometimes called "the Olympics of hula." Hula is the traditional dance of the Hawaiian people.

FAST FACTS

CAPITAL Honolulu

FUNNY PLACE NAMES
Captain Cook, Cod Fish Village, Elevenmile Homestead, Haiku, Happy Valley, Volcano

STATE SLANG
• The friendly "ALOHA" means either hello or goodbye, as well as love and compassion. "MAHALO" is "thank you."

• ONO GRINDS is delicious-tasting food.

FANTASTIC FOODS
• SHAVE ICE is similar to a snow cone, except the ice is shaved not crushed, and drenched with flavored syrup.

• POKE is marinated raw fish (usually tuna) cut into cubes and served over rice.

• LAULAU is pork wrapped in taro leaves and cooked in an underground hot rock oven for hours until it's soft and smoky flavored.

COOL INVENTIONS
• SURFING was called "wave sliding," when it started thousands of years ago in Hawaii. Early surfboards made of solid wood weighed more than 150 pounds, were 10–16 feet long, and didn't have a fin. Olympic swimmer Duke Kahanamoku popularized the sport around the world in the early 1900s.

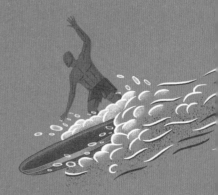

BOOKS *Aloha, Kanani* by Lisa Yee • *Attack on Pearl Harbor (Ranger in Time)* by Kate Messner

State Favorites

DESSERT haupia • **COOKIE** white chocolate macadamia nut • **MUFFIN** coconut

Hawaii is one of only two states that grow COFFEE. (The other is California.)

You can MAIL A COCONUT from Hawaii. No box. No packaging. Just write the address on the coconut. Really.

KALAUNU Nº274

The Big Island has over 600 MACADAMIA NUT farms. Macadamias have the hardest shell and are the most expensive to buy of any nut.

There are only 13 letters in the HAWAIIAN ALPHABET: A, E, I, O, U, H, K, L, M, N, P, W, plus the apostrophe, or okina, which is used as a letter.

Punalu'u BLACK SAND Beach gets its color from lava particles.

The islands' enormous BANYAN TREES aren't native to Hawaii. The first was a gift from India. It was planted in 1873 in the center of Lahaina and is now the state's oldest and largest banyan.

The STATE QUARTER features Hawaiian KING KAMEHAMEHA I stretching his hand toward the Hawaiian ISLANDS. In the early 1800s, he united the islands into one kingdom.

HAWAII 1959
UA MAU KE EA O KA AINA I KA PONO

The Spouting Horn BLOWHOLE in Koloa sends the ocean water 50 feet into the air with a hissing sound. Local legend says it's caused by a lizard monster trapped in a lava tube under the ocean!

Hawaiians love SPAM! They eat over 7 million cans a year, way more than any other state. It's on Hawaii's McDonald's and Burger King menus, and you can try Spam ice cream and Spam French fries at the Waikiki Spam Jam festival on Oahu!

Hold a SEAHORSE in your hand at the Ocean Rider Seahorse Farm in Kona. A baby seahorse is called a fry.

Almost every morning, RAINBOWS appear in Waianuenue (Rainbow Falls) in Hilo. The waterfall flows over a lava cave that according to legends is home to the ancient Hawaiian goddess Hina.

It's against state law to put up a BILLBOARD.

Snorkle with GIANT MANTA RAYS in the waters off the Big Island! Did you know manta rays have the largest known brains of any fish?

The state fish is the HUMUHUMUNUKUNUKUAPUA'A, which means "triggerfish with a snout like a pig." Despite its lengthy name, this fish is only about 10 inches long.

If you measure from its base on the sea floor up to its top, MAUNA LOA on the Big Island is the world's largest VOLCANO and mountain—in total, a mile taller than Mount Everest!

You'd think Idaho would be called the "Potato State" because it grows about 13 billion pounds of potatoes a year, but its official nickname is the "Gem State." More than 72 different precious and semi-precious gemstones have been mined here— only Africa has a bigger variety of gems. Plus, Idaho is one of only two places in the world (the other's in India) where the rare star garnet (a deep-red gemstone) can be found.

SPUD-TACULAR FUN!

See the world's largest POTATO CHIP "crisp" (a 25-inch Pringle) at the Idaho Potato Museum in Blackfoot (where every out-of-stater gets a free tater!).

One of Idaho's most popular hotels is a ONE-ROOM, 6-TON POTATO!

Ring in New Year's with a huge glowing fake potato at the IDAHO POTATO DROP in Boise (locals say BOY-SEE, never BOY-ZEE).

Go to the movies and pose with a giant fake potato at the SPUD DRIVE-IN THEATER in Driggs.

The Gem State

iDAHO

Idaho has the only STATE SEAL designed by a woman. Created in 1891, during the women's suffrage movement (fight for the right to vote), Emma Edwards Green placed a woman with the scales of justice next to a male miner.

The largest human-tamed GEYSER is in Soda Springs.

In 1936, Sun Valley Resort—the first SKI RESORT in the U.S.—began operating the world's first CHAIRLIFT.

At 7,993 feet, Hell's Canyon is the DEEPEST GORGE in America— deeper than the Grand Canyon!

Nature's giant sandbox! Bruneau Dunes State Park has the tallest free-standing SAND DUNE in the U.S.

The Boise State Broncos were the first U.S. university team to play on a non-green football field. They call their BLUE FIELD the Smurf Turf!

STATE Favorites

CANDY Owyhee Idaho Spud bar · PIZZA TOPPING black olives · DESSERT ice cream potato

FAST FACTS

CAPITAL Boise

FUNNY PLACE NAMES Atomic City, Cocolalla, Cold House, Good Grief, Gross, Headquarters, Magic City, Riddle, Slickpoo, Squirrel, Sugar City, Waha

STATE SLANG

• When Idahoans ask you to "pass the FRY SAUCE," they're looking to dip their French fries in a special sauce made with ketchup and mayonnaise.

• A JOCKEY BOX is a car's glove compartment.

• Ground squirrels are sometimes called WHISTLE PIGS.

The **STATE QUARTER** features the state outline and a PEREGRINE FALCON, the world's fastest animal. These speedy raptors reach over 200 miles per hour in a dive. Watch one soar at the Peregrine Fund's World Center for Birds of Prey in Boise.

FANTASTIC FOODS

• FINGER STEAKS—batter-fried strips of steak served with a tangy sauce—are said to have been created in Boise.

• HUCKLEBERRY PIE is a summertime favorite. Huckleberries—a tiny, tart purple berry—were made the state fruit thanks to a fourth-grade class.

COOL INVENTIONS

• In high school chemistry class in Rigby, 14-year-old Philo T. Farnsworth sketched an idea for a vacuum tube to allow pictures to be televised electronically. By the time he was 21 in 1927, Farnsworth had created the first working all-electric TELEVISION.

BOOKS *Walk Two Moons* by Sharon Creech • *My Life As a Potato* by Arianne Costner

Boise City Hall is geothermally heated from UNDERGROUND HOT SPRINGS.

Celebrate SACAGAWEA Heritage Days in Salmon. Born in Idaho into the Agaidika Lemhi Shoshone tribal nation, 16-year-old Sacagawea was a member of explorers Lewis and Clark's cross-country expedition to the Pacific Ocean.

The U.S. Navy tests SUBMARINES in the very deep and quiet waters of Lake Pend Oreille.

Spend the night in the doghouse! Dog Bark Park Inn in Cottonwood has a 30-foot-tall BEAGLE BED AND BREAKFAST!

In 1928, a Hagerman cattle rancher discovered FOSSIL BONES that were 3 million years old. They were from a zebra-like animal known as the Hagerman horse and are now on display at the Hagerman Fossil Beds National Monument.

Walk the nation's LONGEST MAIN STREET (33 miles!) in Island Park.

Orofino LUMBERJACK Days celebrate the logging industry with sawing, chopping, and pole-climbing contests.

Over 1,500 SHEEP parade the streets of Ketchum on their way to winter pastures at the annual Trailing of the Sheep Festival.

Get the dirt about the history and art of staying clean at the MUSEUM OF CLEAN in Pocatello.

ILLINOIS

The Prairie State

The Land of Lincoln

The world's largest ROCKING CHAIR is in Casey. At over 56 feet tall, it takes 10 people to rock it.

METROPOLIS is the home of SUPERMAN and the Super Museum filled with "Man of Steel" memorabilia, and, of course, an outdoor phone booth.

Known as LITTLE EGYPT, three towns in southern Illinois are named Cairo, Thebes, and Karnak. The Southern Illinois University mascot is the Saluki, an ancient breed of Egyptian hunting dog.

Findlay has the only GOAT TOWER in the U.S. The spiral stairs wrapped around the 31-foot-tall "tower of BAAA" acts as a playground for goats!

Enjoy BURGOO, a savory pioneer stew cooked for 18 hours over a wood fire at the Burgoo Festival in Utica. Originally made with squirrel, today's stew uses beef instead.

The Chicago River FLOWS BACKWARD! And on St. Patrick's Day, it's dyed GREEN.

The International Museum of Surgical Science in Chicago has an AMPUTATION DEMONSTRATION!

CATSU

The world's largest BOTTLE OF CATSUP is a 170-foot tall water tower in Collinsville. Never put catsup (also spelled ketchup) on a hotdog in Chicago —only mustard!

Morton calls itself the PUMPKIN Capital of the World because more than 85% of canned pumpkin is processed here.

State Favorites   SNACK cheddar and caramel popcorn • PIE pumpkin • PIZZA TOPPING sausage

Illinois boasts a little bit of everything and everyone. It's thought to be the most "typically American" of any state, with a population representing the different attitudes, beliefs, and cultures of Americans. Illinois is made up of family farms and orchards, the big-city bustle of Chicago, the Shawnee National Forest, and miles of beach alongside Lake Michigan.

The TALLEST MAN in recorded history, Robert Pershing Wadlow, was born in Alton. He stood 8 feet, 11 inches tall and wore a size 37 shoe!

The SMALLEST CAT on record lived in Taylorville in the 1990s. The tiny feline was just 2.75 inches tall!

When the first DAIRY QUEEN opened in Joliet in 1940, a soft serve cone cost a nickel!

Both the Freeport and New Berlin schools have a PRETZEL as their mascot.

The first SOFTBALL game was played in Chicago on Thanksgiving Day, 1887, using a boxing glove as a ball and a broom as a bat. The game was called indoor baseball, kitten ball, lemon ball, and mush ball, before officially becoming softball in 1926.

Sign up for the junior LOGSPLITTING competition at the Abraham Lincoln National Railsplitting Festival in Lincoln.

FAST FACTS

CAPITAL Springfield

FUNNY PLACE NAMES Cave-in-Rock, Chicken Bristle, Crisp, Disco, Fishhook, Frog City, Goofy Ridge, Grand Detour, Half Day, Muddy, Normal, Oblong

STATE SLANG
• Chicagoans call athletic shoes **GYM SHOES**, not "sneakers" or "tennis shoes."

• In Chicago, the living room is often called the **FRUNCHROOM**. The room with the toilet and the bathtub is the **WASHROOM**.

The STATE QUARTER features a young **ABRAHAM LINCOLN** (who moved to Illinois at age 21) between a farm and the Chicago skyline. Illinois has the most "Honest Abe" sites to visit in the nation.

FANTASTIC FOODS
• **CHICAGO-STYLE DEEP DISH PIZZA** is baked in a deep skillet and assembled with the sauce on top of the gooey cheese. The only way to eat it is with a knife and fork!

• The **HORSESHOE** (an open-faced sandwich from Springfield) is a hamburger patty on thick, toasted bread, smothered in cheese sauce, and piled with crispy French fries.

COOL INVENTIONS
• The first working **CELL PHONE** was invented by Motorola's Martin Cooper in Schaumburg in 1973. It took 10 more years for it to be sold in stores—and cost nearly $4,000 per phone!

• **TWINKIES** were created by James Dewar for the Continental Baking Company in Schiller Park in 1930. Originally the snack cakes had banana filling, but this was switched to vanilla when bananas were rationed during World War II.

BOOKS *Finding Langston* by Lesa Cline-Ransome • *The First Rule of Punk* by Celia C. Pérez

No one knows for sure why Indiana is called the "Hoosier State." Some say it's from frontier days, when travelers approached someone's cabin and the cabin owner called out a friendly "Who's here?", but it sounded like "Who's yere?" which then became "Hoosier." Indiana continues to welcome travelers: with its central location and major Interstate highways, its state motto is the "Crossroads of America."

Take a tiny peek at the eensy-weensy houses on display at the Museum of MINIATURE HOUSES in Carmel.

It's against state law to catch a FISH with your bare hands.

The East Race Waterway in South Bend, the first ARTIFICIAL WHITEWATER RAFTING course in the U.S., has six-foot-high waves!

INDIANA
THE HOOSIER STATE

Try spicy, sweet persimmon pudding at the Persimmon Festival in Mitchell. A PERSIMMON is a small orange fruit that tastes like pumpkin.

Indiana University is home to the world's largest anatomically correct SCULPTURE OF THE HUMAN BRAIN. The brain weighs 10,000 pounds and is built out of Indiana limestone.

Slide into one of the world's largest TOILETS in Columbus!

Visitors can add a layer to one of the tens of thousands of coats of paint on the world's largest BALL OF PAINT in Alexandria.

The first professional BASEBALL GAME was played in Fort Wayne on May 4th, 1871.

State Favorites

BREAKFAST biscuits and gravy · VEGETABLE broccoli · SNACK popcorn

The INDY 500 automobile race draws the biggest crowd of any sporting event. The 33-car race is held every May, and it's a tradition that the winning driver chugs a bottle of chilled milk.

A few days before the Indy 500, the Indianapolis Zoo hosts a TORTOISE RACE. The (much slower) winner also gets milk at the finish line (but a person drinks it for the tortoise).

Miki Sudo set the world record at the Indiana State Fair in 2017 by eating 16.5 gallons of ICE CREAM in only six minutes.

Home to 31 COVERED BRIDGES, Parke County is called the Covered Bridge Capital of the World.

The world's record for the largest collection of COOKIE JARS (2,653) belongs to Edith Eva Fuchs of Metamora.

Every year, thousands of letters to jolly St. Nick are mailed to the SANTA CLAUS post office: 45 North Kringle Place, Santa Claus, Indiana 47579.

The LEVI COFFIN HOUSE in Fountain City has been called the "Grand Central Station of the Underground Railroad." From 1827 to 1842, Quakers Levi and Catharine Coffin sheltered an estimated 2,000 men, women, and children escaping slavery.

FAST FACTS

CAPITAL Indianapolis

FUNNY PLACE NAMES Bean Blossom, Beehunter, Correct, Daylight, Gnaw Bone, Popcorn, Raccoon, Santa Claus, Toad Hop, Young America

STATE SLANG
- Green peppers are often called **MANGOES**.
- Indianans say **"OPE!"** instead of "oops" or "uh-oh!"
- "Please, sweep your room," doesn't mean grab a broom. A vacuum is called a **SWEEPER** here.

The **STATE QUARTER** features **19 STARS** (Indiana was the 19th state) and a **RACECAR**. Ray Harroun won the first Indianapolis 500 in 1911 and also created the first rearview mirror! Harroun attached a mirror to his dashboard, so he could drive a single-seater and still see behind, instead of having a passenger keep look-out.

FANTASTIC FOODS
- The recipe for **SUGAR CREAM PIE** dates back to 1816. This creamy dessert is also called Hoosier Pie, finger pie (you can mix it with your fingers), and desperation pie (you don't need any fruit to make it). Wick's Pies in Winchester bakes up to 10,000 sugar cream pies a day!

- The **PORK TENDERLOIN SANDWICH'S** enormous breaded cutlet extends way beyond the edges of the bun.

- **PUPPY CHOW** is for people, not dogs! The sweet snack is Chex cereal coated in chocolate, peanut butter, and confectioner's sugar.

COOL INVENTIONS
- In 1874, William Blackstone gave his wife a birthday present—a machine that would remove dirt and wash clothing. It was the first **WASHING MACHINE** designed to be used at home.

BOOKS *Running Out of Time* by Margaret Peterson Haddix • *The Season of Styx Malone* by Kekla Magoon

The Iowa State Fair is a huge deal in this state where farms cover most of the land. Every August, over a million people gather for rides, games, foods-on-a-stick, hog hollerin' contests, and livestock competitions (the biggest boar weighed in at 1,335 pounds!). The main attraction is always a 600-pound cow made of butter. Can you guess how many slices of toast you could butter with that cow? About 19,200!

iOWA

The Hawkeye State

It's against state law to call or market imitation butter or margarine as real BUTTER.

Play with the tiny tractors and silos at the National FARM TOY Museum in Dyersville.

Snake Alley in Burlington competes with Lombard Street in San Francisco, CA for the title of MOST CROOKED STREET IN THE WORLD. While Lombard has more turns, Snake Alley's are more extreme.

Iowa resident Hans Nilsen Langseth set the record for the LONGEST BEARD in 1927. At 17 feet, 6 inches long, his beard was nearly the length of three beds!

Iowa has more PIGS and HOGS than people!

The world's largest POPCORN BALL in Sac City weighs a sweet 9,370 pounds.

Legend says if an Iowa State University student steps on the BRONZE ZODIAC RELIEF on the floor of the Memorial Union, they'll fail their next exam.

RAGBRAI (the *Register*'s Annual Great Bicycle Ride Across Iowa) is the largest BIKE-TOURING EVENT in the world. Thousands of cyclists pedal across the entire state.

The Fenelon Place Elevator in Dubuque is described as the world's SHORTEST, STEEPEST SCENIC RAILWAY (also called a funicular).

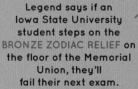

State Favorites

PIZZA TOPPING bacon • BREAKFAST monkey bread

FAST FACTS

CAPITAL Des Moines

FUNNY PLACE NAMES
Beebeetown, Cool, Defiance, Gravity, Hard Scratch, Last Chance, Lone Tree, Lost Nation, Unique, What Cheer

STATE SLANG
• **"KNEE-HIGH BY THE FOURTH OF JULY"** is a saying to measure the success of the corn crop. Decades ago, farmers wanted their stalks to reach this height by Independence Day. Today, due to advances in farming, corn grows much taller.

The **STATE QUARTER** features a painting of a teacher and students planting a tree near a schoolhouse. The painting is by Iowa artist **GRANT WOOD**, whose most famous painting, of a pitchfork-holding farmer and a woman, is called *American Gothic*.

FANTASTIC FOODS
• The **MAID RITE** is a loose meat sandwich (like a sloppy joe minus the tomato sauce).

• Iowa grows more corn than any other state, and **SWEET CORN ON THE COB** is enjoyed seasoned with salt or smeared with butter.

• Mix marshmallow krispie treats with creamy peanut butter, milk chocolate, and butterscotch chips, and you get **SCOTCHAROOS**. These yummy bars are served at Iowa picnics and barbecues.

COOL INVENTIONS
• In the 1930s, University of Iowa gymnastics champ George Nissen built a "bouncing rig" with scrap steel, tire inner tubes, and canvas. He called it a **TRAMPOLINE** after the Spanish word for "diving board." To help sell it, he gave a demonstration jumping with a kangaroo!

BOOKS *Dewey the Library Cat* by Vicki Myron with Bret Witter • *The Luck of the Buttons* by Anne Ylvisaker

Vikings and trolls fill the streets of Decorah's **NORDIC FEST.**

Graduates of the **IOWA WRITERS' WORKSHOP,** the oldest creative writing degree program in the U.S., have won 17 Pulitzer Prizes.

Celebrate Dutch culture with over 80,000 blooming **TULIPS** at the Tulip Time Festival in Pella.

Le Mars, home of Blue Bunny **ICE CREAM,** calls itself the Ice Cream Capital of the World.

Lisbon Sauerkraut Days isn't all fermented cabbage (that's how **SAUERKRAUT** is made). The festival has **BATHTUB RACES,** where one person sits inside a tub on wheels that's pushed by teammates down a racecourse as onlookers throw water balloons!

The world's largest **TRUCK STOP** is in Walcott. It has a store, barber shop, dentist, laundromat, pet bath, library, workout room, movie theater, and the Iowa 80 Trucking Museum.

Hundreds of ancient Indigenous burial and ceremonial mounds make up the **EFFIGY MOUNDS NATIONAL MONUMENT.**

In the 1870s, a farmer in Peru, Iowa, tried unsuccessfully to cut down the same tree three times. When he finally allowed it to sprout, it produced a new kind of apple—RED DELICIOUS.

ICE CREAM FLAVOR rocky road

Sumner County grows more WHEAT than any place and is known as the Wheat Capital of the World.

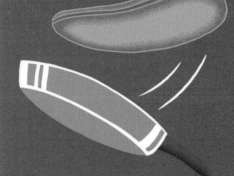

Every Shrove Tuesday (Fat Tuesday or Mardis Gras) since 1950, women from the town of Liberal compete against women in Olney, England, in a 415-yard International PANCAKE DAY RACE. They flip pancakes in a skillet while sprinting through each town.

Experience life as it once was in the ultimate OLD WEST town of Dodge City, where Wyatt Earp was sheriff.

It's against state law to SCREECH YOUR TIRES when you drive.

There's a GRASSHOPPER CHURCH in Hutchinson! Built during the grasshopper (Rocky Mountain locust) plague of 1874, the First United Methodist Church has thousands of grasshoppers mixed into its foundation. The insect swarms were so large they blocked the sun.

Kansas has the nation's largest population of PRAIRIE CHICKENS. Speaking of chickens—in 1928, a tornado in Kansas plucked the feathers off some chickens!

FAST FACTS

CAPITAL Topeka

FUNNY PLACE NAMES
Beagle, Bird City, Buttermilk, Elmo, Gas, Gross, Protection, Skiddy, Smileyberg

STATE SLANG:
• If something is CADDY-CORNER or CATTY-CORNER, it's diagonal from you.

• If someone orders a CONCRETE, they want a super-thick frozen custard blended with toppings.

The **STATE QUARTER** features an AMERICAN BISON and SUNFLOWERS. Twenty million American bison once roamed the Great Plains, before white settlers hunted them and built on the land. The tall, yellow sunflower still grows wild here and is used to make sunflower oil—and sunflower seeds to snack on!

KANSAS 1861

FANTASTIC FOODS
• Kansas loves BARBECUE! Racks of smoked pork or beef ribs are smothered in a tangy, thick molasses and tomato-based sauce.

• Dynamic duo! CHILI AND CINNAMON ROLLS are served together here.

COOL INVENTIONS
• The first PIZZA HUT was opened in Wichita in 1958. Two brothers in college borrowed $600 from their mother to start the business.

• Forest P. Gill, a silkscreen printer from Kansas City, created the first adhesive BUMPER STICKERS in the 1940s. Before this, people used wire and string to attach homemade signs to their car's bumper.

BOOKS
May B. by Caroline Starr Rose • *Moon Over Manifest* by Clare Vanderpool

BIG BRUTUS in West Mineral is the world's largest electric coal shovel. Southeast Kansas was once a busy coal-mining area.

The FIRST WOMAN MAYOR in the U.S. was Susanna Salter. A group of men in Argonia put her name on the ballot as a prank, assuming she'd lose and discourage local women from politics. Much to their surprise, she won the 1887 election and became mayor!

State Favorites
PIE sour cream and raisin • HALLOWEEN CANDY Reese's Peanut Butter Cups • SNACK hamburger

KANSAS

The Sunflower State

"Toto, I've a feeling we're not in Kansas anymore," Dorothy tells her dog in the famous movie *The Wizard of Oz*. After a tornado carries her to a magical world, all Dorothy wants is to go home to her beloved Kansas with its wide, flat fields of amber wheat. Today, in Kansas, you can follow the yellow brick road to the world's largest display of Oz artifacts at the Oz Museum, enter your dog in the Toto look-alike contest at OZtoberfest in Wamego, and even visit a replica of Dorothy's farmhouse in Liberal.

The world's largest HAIRBALL (called a trichobezoar) weighed 55 pounds when it was removed from the stomach of a cow in Garden City.

The BARBED WIRE Museum in La Crosse has 2,000 kinds of barbed wire. Competitors at the World Champion Barbed Wire Splicing Contest try to mend a fence fastest with the tightest splice (joining wires together).

Ride an antique CAROUSEL at the C.W. Parker Carousel Museum in Leavenworth.

About 250,000 children rode what was called the ORPHAN TRAIN across the country from 1854 to 1929. At farm towns, they were taken off to be chosen by families. Those not chosen were sent on to the next stations. The National Orphan Train Complex in Concordia tells their stories.

An enormous EASEL in Goodland displays a replica (copy) of one of Vincent Van Gogh's *Sunflower* paintings.

At night, bonfires form a ring of fire around the 44-foot-tall KEEPER OF THE PLAINS steel statue in Wichita, which honors the region's many Indigenous tribes.

The world's largest BALL OF TWINE in Cawker City weighs more than 27,000 pounds and is still growing.

FAST FACTS

CAPITAL Frankfort

FUNNY PLACE NAMES Barefoot, Bee Lick, Dog Walk, Lickskillet, Monkey's Eyebrow, Ordinary, Oven Fork, Paint Lick, Parrot, Pig, Possum Trot, Rabbit Hash, Shoulderblade, Snow, Typo

STATE SLANG

• If someone orders a **HOT BROWN** with **ALE-8**, they want the famous Louisville turkey and bacon open-face sandwich smothered in creamy Mornay sauce and an Ale-8-One, the local ginger-citrus soda.

• Don't put a sled on your head if you're told to wear a **TOBOGGAN**. A toboggan is a knitted snow hat.

The **STATE QUARTER** features a **THOROUGHBRED RACEHORSE** and the house that inspired Stephen Foster to write the state song, "My Old Kentucky Home." At the Kentucky Derby, only three-year-old Thoroughbreds compete.

FANTASTIC FOODS

• **DERBY PIE** is filled with chocolate chips and walnuts or pecans and enjoyed on Kentucky Derby day.

• **APPLE STACK CAKE** is a specialty of Appalachia. According to legend, early mountain settlers couldn't afford fancy wedding cakes, so neighbors would each donate a thin cake layer, and the bride's family would spread applesauce or apple butter to stack the layers. The number of layers in the finished cake told how popular the bride was!

COOL INVENTIONS

• The song **"HAPPY BIRTHDAY TO YOU"** is believed to have been written by two Louisville sisters in 1893.

• In 1884, 17-year-old John Hillerich created the first custom-made **BASEBALL BAT** for Louisville's star player in his father's woodworking shop. When the player went three-for-three, everyone wanted a "Louisville Slugger" bat! The world's largest bat (120 feet tall) now stands outside the Louisville Slugger Museum.

BOOKS *Chasing Redbird* by Sharon Creech • *Becoming Muhammad Ali* by James Patterson and Kwame Alexander

Mammoth Cave National Park is the world's longest known CAVE SYSTEM, with more than 400 miles of underground passageways.

The ABRAHAM LINCOLN LOOK-ALIKE CONTEST takes place in Hodgenville, where the 16th president was born in a log cabin in 1809.

Ka-boom! THUNDER OVER LOUISVILLE, the opening ceremony for the Kentucky Derby, is one of the largest annual FIREWORK displays in the country.

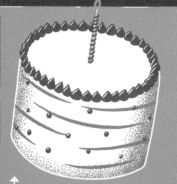

Racing champions live out their senior years at the OLD FRIENDS THOROUGHBRED RETIREMENT FARM in Georgetown.

"Float like a butterfly, sting like a bee." Cave Hill Cemetery in Louisville, burial place of boxing legend MUHAMMAD ALI, sells HONEY produced from its own hives.

In 2018, champion eater Joey Chestnut set a world's record by eating 81 mutton (sheep meat) sandwiches in 10 minutes at the MUTTON GLUTTON contest in Owensboro.

Every year, Kentuckians hold a 400-MILE YARD SALE with thousands of bargains set up along historic Highway 68.

STATE Favorites
VEGETABLE summer squash • **BREAKFAST** country ham biscuits • **SNACK** cheese dip and pretzels

KENTUCKY

THE BLUEGRASS STATE

Kentucky is horse country, with rolling-hill equine farms, training centers, and race tracks covering the state. On the first Saturday in May, a bugle signals the start of the Kentucky Derby, the world's most-watched horse race—known as "the most famous two minutes in sports." The winning horse is covered with a heavy blanket of over 400 red roses.

In 1938, Bill Monroe and his band the Blue Grass Boys started BLUEGRASS MUSIC, which often features a fiddle, banjo, guitar, mandolin, and upright bass.

Nearly 1,000 dummies sit staring in rows at the Vent Haven Museum in Fort Mitchell, the world's only museum of VENTRILOQUISM.

In the spring, bluish buds bloom in the fields, giving the grass a blue tint—that's why Kentucky's known as the BLUEGRASS STATE.

GOLD BARS worth several hundred billion dollars are stored in underground vaults located in Fort Knox.

Middlesboro is the only known U.S. city built inside a METEOR CRATER.

Louisville is one of the world's largest producers of DISCO BALLS. In the 1970s, it made 90% of them!

The International Museum of the HORSE in Lexington is the largest museum dedicated to the history of the human/horse connection.

The MOTHER GOOSE HOUSE in Hazard is shaped like a goose sitting on a nest.

Lake Cumberland is known as the HOUSEBOAT Capital of the World.

The MARY TODD LINCOLN HOUSE in Lexington, childhood home of Abe's wife, was the country's first house museum to honor a First Lady.

LOUISIANA

Louisiana is a musical mixing pot of so many beats and melodies. Jazz got its start in New Orleans and was made popular by Louis "Satchmo" Armstrong. Zydeco was created by Black Creole sharecroppers and farmers in southwestern Louisiana. It combines French accordion tunes, Afro-Caribbean beats, and blues. Lively folk-inspired Cajun music was introduced by the Acadians, who moved to Louisiana after being forced out of Nova Scotia in the 1700s. And that's not all—brass, blues, rhythm and blues, gospel, country, and swamp pop have lots of Louisiana in them too!

The Pelican State

The ROUGAROU Fest in Houma celebrates the Cajun legend of the Rougarou, a werewolf-like creature said to live in the BAYOUS (slow-moving creeks or swampy lakes).

At the Rig Museum (International Petroleum Museum & Exposition) in Morgan City, you can tour "Mr. Charlie," an OFFSHORE DRILLING RIG once used in the Gulf of Mexico. Oil and gas are important Louisiana industries.

The Lake Pontchartrain Causeway Bridge is the LONGEST BRIDGE over continuous water in the world. It's almost 24 miles long!

Called the CRAWFISH Capital of the World, Breaux Bridge hosts an annual Crawfish Festival. Freshwater crawfish look like baby lobsters and are eaten steamed or boiled.

Want to see FROGS race wearing fancy costumes? Hop over to the Frog Festival in Rayne. The town was once one of the biggest restaurant suppliers of frog legs.

See ya later! Louisiana has the largest ALLIGATOR population. Over 2 million live in the state's wetlands and lakes.

SHRIMP AND ALLIGATOR CHEESECAKE is served in some restaurants throughout the state.

State Favorites

COOKIE maple pecan · FRUIT strawberries · PIZZA TOPPING peppers

FAST FACTS

CAPITAL Baton Rouge

FUNNY PLACE NAMES Cranky Corner, Cut Off, Grosse Tête ("Big Head"), Happy Jack, Lucky, Start, Uneedus, Waterproof

STATE SLANG

"WHERE YAT?" means "How are you doing? What have you been up to?"

"LAISSEZ LES BONS TEMPS ROULER!" is a French phrase meaning "Let the good times roll!"

The **STATE QUARTER** features the BROWN PELICAN (the state bird), a TRUMPET, and an outline of the LOUISIANA PURCHASE territory, which the U.S. bought from France in 1803 for $15 million. Called "the greatest real estate deal in history," the Purchase doubled the size of the nation.

FANTASTIC FOODS

It's a tasty showdown in Louisiana! Which do you choose?

JAMBALAYA, a spicy rice- and meat-based hearty stew, OR GUMBO, a thick, spicy soup made with okra and either sausage, chicken, or seafood served with rice. Both are cooked with the Louisiana "trinity": celery, peppers, and onions.

MUFFULETTA, a round Italian sandwich filled with a variety of meats and olive salad, OR PO'BOY (poor boy), a long sandwich on French bread stuffed with fried seafood (often oysters or shrimp) or roast beef. Order it "dressed," and you'll get lettuce, tomatoes, pickles, and mayo.

BEIGNETS, square doughnuts covered with powdered sugar OR PRALINES, patty-shaped candy made of sugar, butter, cream, and pecans.

COOL INVENTIONS

Sarah Breedlove was born near Delta and known professionally as MADAM C.J. WALKER. She invented a line of hair products for Black women. They were so incredibly popular that Madam C.J. Walker became the country's first self-made female millionaire.

The famous TABASCO hot sauce, invented by Edmund McIlhenny on Avery Island in 1868, has just three ingredients: tabasco peppers, salt, and vinegar. Visitors can tour the factory where 700,000 bottles are produced each day and walk the fields where the spicy peppers are grown.

BOOKS *My Louisiana Sky* by Kimberly Willis Holt
Bayou Magic by Jewell Parker Rhodes

The Touchstone Wildlife & Art Museum in Haughton is stuffed with unique TAXIDERMIED ANIMALS.

The silvery-gray SPANISH MOSS hanging from tree branches throughout the state is an epiphyte, a plant that absorbs all nutrients from the air and doesn't harm the tree it grows on.

Louisiana is the only state with PARISHES instead of counties.

At the Abbeville GIANT OMELETTE Celebration, chefs crack over 5,000 eggs to cook an enormous omelette.

Ready, set, paddle at the World Champion Jean Lafitte Pirogue Races. Called the "Cajun canoe," the long, skinny PIROGUE was built to navigate the shallow swamps and bayous.

The New Orleans Pharmacy Museum sits inside the apothecary of America's first LICENSED PHARMACIST and is filled with old-time curiosities, such as leech jars, odd surgical tools, and a soda fountain.

With its rocky coastlines and majestic pine forests, Maine harvests the most lobsters and grows the most blueberries in the country. Did you know lobsters are green, yellow, or blue in the ocean and only turn red when cooked? And blueberries are one of only a few foods that are naturally blue in color?

Maine is the only state with a ONE-SYLLABLE NAME.

Eastport is the EASTERNMOST U.S. city, but on New Year's Day, Cadillac Mountain on Mount Desert Island sees the FIRST SUNRISE of the year.

THE PINE TREE STATE
MAINE

The International CRYPTOZOOLOGY Museum in Portland showcases mysterious creatures, such as the Abominable Snowman and lake monsters.

Every February 14th for over 40 years, Portland woke up to hundreds of mysterious red paper hearts all over the city. The identity of the so-called VALENTINE'S DAY BANDIT—Kevin Fahrman—was revealed after he died in 2023.

MOXIE is the official soft drink of Maine. The beloved bitter-tasting beverage is celebrated at the three-day Moxie Festival in Lisbon.

The UMBRELLA COVER Museum on Peaks Island holds the world's record for the most umbrella sleeves.

Lenny is a 1,700-pound MILK CHOCOLATE MOOSE that lives inside a candy store in Scarborough. He's reportedly the world's largest chocolate animal sculpture.

The giant BLUEBERRY-shaped Wild Blueberry Land in Columbia Falls has a big bakery and a blueberry-themed mini-golf course!

The Maine Coast SARDINE History Museum in Jonesport is all about the salty little fishes.

COOKIE molasses · ICE CREAM FLAVOR chocolate · SNACK Humpty Dumpty BBQ chips

Vacationland

The MAINE COON CAT is one of the largest domestic cat breeds. Its shaggy coat keeps it warm in Maine's frigid winters, and the fur on the cat's paws acts like built-in snowshoes.

Every July, the Central Maine Egg Festival gets cooking in a 10-foot, 300-pound FRYING PAN.

WIGGLY BRIDGE in York is the country's smallest suspension bridge. Legend has it a Girl Scout troop named the bouncy bridge "wiggly" when they walked over it.

EARTHA, the world's largest revolving and rotating globe, spins in Yarmouth.

The world's largest WHOOPIE PIE was created in South Portland in 2011 and weighed 1,062 pounds. A whoopie pie (the official state treat) is two soft cookie-cakes filled with thick frosting.

MASHED POTATO WRESTLING is spuds of fun at the Maine Potato Blossom Festival in Fort Fairfield.

FAST FACTS

CAPITAL Augusta

FUNNY PLACE NAMES Bald Head, Beans Corner, Burnt Porcupine Island, Cape Porpoise, Limerick, Misery Gore, Mistake Island

STATE SLANG

• If you're **FROM AWAY,** you're not from Maine.

• "**AYUH,** my shoes are in the **DOORYARD,**" means "Yes, my shoes are in the front yard."

The **STATE QUARTER** features the **LIGHTHOUSE** at Pemaquid Point and a **SCHOONER** (a sailboat with two or more masts) at sea. There are about 60 lighthouses on Maine's coastline and harbors.

FANTASTIC FOODS

• **LOBSTER ROLLS** in Maine are made with chunks of fresh lobster mixed with mayo and served cold on a split top bun.

• **POTATO CANDY** is a dark chocolate candy with mashed potato and coconut in the center.

• **FIDDLEHEAD FERNS** grow near rivers and lakes. The coiled fiddleheads look like the top of a violin and taste like a combination of asparagus, okra, and spinach.

COOL INVENTIONS

• In the 1870s, 15-year-old Chester Greenwood of Farmington was ice skating when his ears got cold. He had his grandmother attach beaver fur to a wire frame and invented the first **EARMUFFS**!

• The first fried doughnuts didn't have holes, so the center was often raw. In 1847, 16-year-old Hansen Gregory from Rockport punched a hole in the center using a round tin box. The doughnut cooked more evenly, and the **RING-SHAPED DOUGHNUT** was born.

BOOKS *Charlotte's Web* by E.B. White • *Echo Mountain* by Lauren Wolk

In Maryland (pronounced "Merlin" or "Marilyn," but never "Mary-land,") blue crabs rule! The state sits on the Chesapeake Bay, one of the best crabbing spots in the country. Locals love the delicate flavor of steamed or boiled crabs dipped in butter, but "cracking crab"—cracking the shells and picking out the tender meat—can be messy business. The scientific name for blue crabs is *Callinectes sapdius*, which means "beautiful savory swimmer." How perfect is that?

It's often said kids in Maryland are born with a lax stick in their hands! First played by Native nations as stickball centuries ago, LACROSSE is the official state team sport. The National Lacrosse Hall of Fame and Museum is in Sparks.

The National in Crisfield, nicknamed the Crab Capital of the World, has crab races and a boat docking contest.

MARYLAND
THE OLD LINE STATE

Crack codes at the National CRYPTOLOGIC Museum in Annapolis Junction, and check out a Civil War code book and World War II Enigma cipher machine.

The Museum of CIVIL WAR MEDICINE in Frederick is more than amputating legs and biting bullets—it shares stories of innovation and healing.

In 1784, the first successful passenger BALLOON FLIGHT in the U.S. took place in Baltimore. Thirteen-year-old Edward Warren was the only one on board!

Maryland is the only state that has NO NATURAL LAKE.

Maryland is often called AMERICA IN MINIATURE because it has four seasons and almost all the different terrains found in the country.

In the Green Mount Cemetery, the gravestone of OUIJA BOARD inventor Elijah Bond was carved to look like a Ouija board!

During the War of 1812, Francis Scott Key wrote the national anthem, "THE STAR-SPANGLED BANNER," while watching the British bomb Fort McHenry in Baltimore Harbor. It's a tradition for Baltimore Orioles' baseball fans to yell the "O" in the line: "Oh say does that Star-Spangled Banner yet wave," when singing the song.

State Favorites
DESSERT Smith Island cake · **SEASONING** Old Bay · **SNACK** Utz "The Crab Chip" potato chips

FAST FACTS

CAPITAL Annapolis

FUNNY PLACE NAMES Accident, Apple Greene, Boring, Funkstown, Hurry, Martin's Additions, Mousetown, Scientists Cliffs, Shady Side, T.B.

STATE SLANG

• **BLUES** are blue crabs. A **JIMMY** is a male (there's a Washington Monument-like shape on its apron, or belly) and a **SALLY** or **SOOK** is a female (there's a Capitol building-like shape on its apron).

• "**ARD**" means "all right."

The **STATE QUARTER** features **WHITE OAK** branches (state tree) and the dome of the Maryland **STATEHOUSE**, a building dating back to 1772. It's the country's largest wooden dome constructed without nails.

FANTASTIC FOODS

• **CRAB CAKES** made with spices and breadcrumbs are served with tangy tartar sauce.

• Baltimore's **BERGER COOKIES** are similar to New York's "black and whites," except these cake-like cookies are only covered with chocolate icing (no vanilla!).

• The **SNOWBALL** is flavored shaved ice served in a cup (egg custard is the #1 flavor) and topped with marshmallow cream.

COOL INVENTIONS

• S. Duncan Black and Alonzo G. Decker (Black + Decker) invented the first **PORTABLE ELECTRIC DRILL** for single person use in 1916.

BOOKS *Seven Stories Up* by Laurel Snyder • *Knight's Castle* by Edward Eager

The Free State

Retrace **HARRIET TUBMAN'S** steps throughout Dorchester County. Maryland-born Tubman, one of the most famous conductors of the Underground Railroad, helped enslaved people escape to freedom in the 1800s. She was also the first woman in American history to lead a military assault!

JOUSTING is the official state sport, and jousting tournaments have taken place here since colonial times.

John Paul Jones, often called the father of the American Navy, is buried beneath the **NAVAL ACADEMY** chapel in Annapolis. His 21-ton marble coffin is covered in sculpted barnacles and supported by **BRONZE DOLPHINS**.

GEORGE WASHINGTON'S DENTURES are on display at the Dr. Samuel D. Harris National Museum of Dentistry in Baltimore. Although it's a popular myth that Washington had "wooden teeth," some of his dentures were actually made from hippopotamus ivory!

Listen for the fluttering of tiny wings at the magical **SUMMER SOLSTICE FAERIE FESTIVAL** at the Marshy Point Nature Center.

The nation's first **UMBRELLA FACTORY** began in Baltimore in 1828, and its motto was: "Born in Baltimore, Raised Everywhere!"

Sitting ducks! The Havre de Grace **DECOY** Museum displays thousands of Chesapeake Bay decoys.

In 2019, the Maryland School for the Blind set the world record for the longest continuous game (25 hours and 30 seconds) of **GOALBALL**, a team sport designed for visually impaired athletes.

The Fluff Festival in Somerville honors the sweet hometown invention of MARSHMALLOW FLUFF. Try a Fluffernutter sandwich—a PB&J with fluff instead of jelly!

The first awful painting in the MUSEUM OF BAD ART came out of a Boston trash can!

The Amazing World of DR. SEUSS Museum in Springfield highlights the work of the famous children's book author. Dr. Seuss was a pen (fake) name used by Theodor Geisel.

LAKE CHARGOGGAGOGGMANCHAUGGAGOGGCHAUBUNAGUNGAMAUGG, also called Webster Lake, is the longest place name in the U.S. (45 letters!). It's a Nipmuc Nation name that roughly means "neutral fishing waters," or "You fish on your side, I'll fish on my side, and nobody fishes in the middle."

January 16th is National Fig Newton Day. The FIG NEWTON—a soft cookie filled with fig jam—was named after the town of Newton.

First played in Worcester in 1880, CANDLEPIN BOWLING is like regular bowling but with little balls without finger holes and skinny pins that look like candles.

The PAPER HOUSE in Rockport is an actual house (furniture too!) constructed entirely out of newspaper.

First run in 1897, the BOSTON MARATHON is the world's oldest annual marathon.

FAST FACTS

CAPITAL Boston

FUNNY PLACE NAMES Belchertown, Braintree, Dogtown, Feeding Hills, Lobsterville, Old Furnace, Sandwich, Teaticket

STATE SLANG
• WICKED is another way of saying "very" or "really"—like "wicked excited!"

The STATE QUARTER features a statue of a Revolutionary War MINUTEMAN. Minutemen were colonists who were ready to fight at a minute's notice. The quarter was designed by a sixth and a seventh grader who won a contest hosted by the governor.

FANTASTIC FOODS
• Thick molasses is the secret to BOSTON BAKED BEANS. The beans date back to the Puritans, who'd make a large pot of sweet beans with salt pork on Saturday and let it sit on the hearth until Sunday, a day their religion didn't allow them to cook.

• BOSTON CREAM PIE is a sponge cake with a custard filling and a chocolate glaze. It was invented at Boston's Parker House Hotel in 1856.

COOL INVENTIONS
• In 1938, Ruth Wakefield—owner of the Toll House Inn in Whitman—chopped a chocolate bar into tiny pieces, added them to her cookie dough, and the CHOCOLATE CHIP COOKIE was born.

• In 1950, William Rosenberg opened the very first DUNKIN' DONUTS (now called DUNKIN') in Quincy. He'd originally called it "Open Kettle," but the name was changed once he saw customers dunking doughnuts into their coffee.

BOOKS Million-Dollar Throw by Mike Lupica • The Line Tender by Kate Allen

MASSACHUSETTS

The Bay State

Summertime on the Massachusetts shore means clam bakes and visits to clam shacks, or grabbing your own rake to go clamming for dinner. The mollusks are the star of New England clam chowder, a thick, cream-based soup chock-full of potatoes, onions, and salt pork (don't even think about adding tomatoes!). On Cape Cod, people take fried clams seriously and debate the best way to serve them. Are you Team Fried Clam Strips or Team Fried Clam Whole Bellies?

Roses are red,
Violets are blue.
Esther Howland lived in Worcester
And made the country's first
VALENTINE'S CARDS too.

The Jacob's Pillow Dance Festival is America's LONGEST-RUNNING DANCE FESTIVAL.

The country's OLDEST WOODEN JAIL is in Barnstable. Built around 1690, it's believed by many to be haunted.

Two friends, two games! BASKETBALL was invented in 1891 by James Naismith in Springfield and was first played with a soccer ball and peach baskets instead of nets. Four years later in Holyoke, his friend William G. Morgan wanted a game with less running than basketball, so he invented VOLLEYBALL. He originally named it "mintonette."

OLD JAIL

Do you dig the 783 SHOVELS at the Shovel Museum at Stonehill College in Easton?

HOOD

The giant HOOD MILK BOTTLE next to the Boston Children's Museum is actually an ice-cream stand. If it were real, the 40-foot tall bottle could hold 58,620 gallons of milk! Do you know what a HOODSIE is? It's the Hood dairy company's beloved little cup of vanilla/chocolate ice cream eaten with a wooden spoon.

State Favorites   MUFFIN corn · JUICE cranberry · SNACK Cape Cod potato chips

FAST FACTS

CAPITAL Lansing

FUNNY PLACE NAMES Bad Axe, Bunny Run Lake, Free Soil, Raisin Center, Slapneck, Vulcan, Witch Lake, Wooden Shoe Village, Zilwaukee

STATE SLANG
• The U.P. is the "Upper Peninsula" (the northern section of the state). The people who live here are known as **YOOPERS**. Yoopers call people who live in the Lower Peninsula, or below the Mackinac Bridge (nicknamed **MIGHTY MAC**), **TROLLS**—because trolls live under bridges— or **FLATLANDERS**.

The **STATE QUARTER** features the five **GREAT LAKES** (Superior, Huron, Ontario, Michigan, Erie). The Great Lakes are the largest freshwater system in the world. Need help remembering the lakes' names? Try the mnemonic **SHO ME**.

FANTASTIC FOODS
• The **PASTY** is a handheld meat pie popular in the U.P. Pasties were introduced by Cornish immigrants working in the state's copper mines.

• The **CONEY DOG** is a beef hot dog slathered with all-meat chili, yellow mustard, diced raw onions, and served in a steamed bun.

• **PACZKI** is a Polish round jelly doughnut eaten on Shrove Tuesday (Fat Tuesday or Mardi Gras), also called Paczki Day in Michigan.

COOL INVENTIONS:
• **VERNOR'S GINGER ALE** was one of of the nation's first soft drinks. According to legend, Detroit pharmacist James Vernor was working on a new beverage in 1862, but had to leave to fight in the Civil War. When he came back four years later, he was surprised to discover the drink he'd stored in a barrel had turned golden in color and developed a yummy gingery taste!

• In 1911, Wayne County road commissioner Edward N. Hines had the idea to paint a line down the center of a road to separate traffic in opposing directions. It was one of the most important advancements in **ROAD SAFETY**.

BOOKS *Bud, Not Buddy* by Christopher Paul Curtis • *American as Paneer Pie* by Supriya Kelkar

You can get a UNICORN-HUNTING LICENSE from Michigan's Lake Superior State University!

In 1965 in Muskegon, Sherman Poppen attached two skis together to create the first surfboard for the snow. He called it the "Snurfer," and it eventually became the SNOWBOARD.

Michigan is the nation's TOP AUTOMOBILE MANUFACTURER. Detroit's nickname is "Motor City," and the "Big Three" are General Motors, Fiat Chrysler, and Ford Motor Company. The auto industry is one of the largest users of ROBOTS to paint, weld, and do assembly-line work.

Find a seat at the world's LONGEST BREAKFAST TABLE for the National Cereal Festival in Battle Creek, birthplace of the cereal industry.

The ARAB AMERICAN NATIONAL MUSEUM in Dearborn is the first and only museum in the U.S. dedicated to telling the Arab American story.

Michigan has the most LIGHTHOUSES of any state.

State Favorites

SOFT DRINK Faygo Redpop • **ICE CREAM FLAVOR** Superman • **SNACK** Better Made potato chips

MICHIGAN

The Great Lakes State

Colon calls itself the MAGIC Capital of the World. Can you guess the school mascot? A rabbit!

A group of fifth graders chose the PAINTED TURTLE to be the state reptile. Painted turtles can hold their breath all winter while hibernating on the bottom of ponds and lakes.

Bring out the bibs! The National BABY FOOD Festival in Fremont features an adult Baby Food Eating Contest—one person is blindfolded and then feeds a jar of baby food to their partner!

A tugboat on the Detroit River is the country's only FLOATING POST OFFICE, delivering mail to the cargo ships.

Michigan is the nation's top producer of tart cherries. Each summer, Traverse City hosts the National Cherry Festival with cherry juice, cherry barbecue sauce, cherry jam, cherry pancakes, cherry hot sauce, and, of course, lots of cherry pie to enjoy. Over in Eau Claire, keep an eye out for the International Cherry Pit-Spitting Championship. Brian "Young Gun" Krause set the record in 2004, sending a cherry pit flying a spit-acular 93 feet, 6.5 inches!

THE WOLVERINE STATE

Car-free Mackinac Island calls itself America's FUDGE Capital and hosts the Mackinac Island Fudge Festival. Michiganders refer to tourists as "fudgies," because almost all visitors to northern Michigan buy fudge.

Who will be crowned the next KING OR QUEEN OF BOLOGNA at Yale Bologna Festival?

Michigan is known as "the MITTEN"—can you guess why? (Clue: Find Michigan on the big map at the beginning of this book!)

Ready, set, quack! It's a race to the finish line for about 2,000 yellow RUBBER DUCKS at the Rubber Ducky Festival in Bellaire.

The De Zwaan (The Swan) Windmill in Holland, Michigan, is the only authentic DUTCH WINDMILL operating in the U.S. It produces whole wheat flour.

FAST FACTS

CAPITAL Saint Paul

FUNNY PLACE NAMES Blue Earth, Castle Danger, Dinkytown, Embarrass, Ham Lake, Lac Qui Parle ("Lake that Speaks"), Sleepy Eye, Welcome

STATE SLANG

• **"YA, SURE, YOU BETCHA,"** means you very much agree.

• **"OH, FER CUTE!"** is said when something's absolutely adorable.

The **STATE QUARTER** features a **LOON**, the state bird, on a **LAKE**. Minnesota is known as the "Land of 10,000 Lakes," but it actually has 11,842 lakes!

FANTASTIC FOODS

• **HOTDISH** is a favorite Minnesota comfort food. The one-dish meal is a mixture of meat, vegetables, cheese, and tater tots held together by canned soup (often cream of mushroom).

• **SAMBUSAS** are fried, meat-filled, triangle-shaped pastries from Somalia. Minneapolis-Saint Paul (the Twin Cities) has the largest Somali population in North America.

• The **IRON RANGE PORKETTA**—a fennel-and-garlic-seasoned pulled pork sandwich—is named after the "iron range," the iron-ore mining districts in the northeastern part of the state.

COOL INVENTIONS

• **WATER SKIING** was invented on Lake Pepin by 18-year-old Ralph Samuelson in 1922. He first tried snow skis, but they made him sink, so he crafted wider skis. He then figured out he needed to lean backward with his ski tips up to stay upright (while being pulled by a motorboat).

BOOKS *Ambassador* by William Alexander • *Brave Like That* by Lindsey Stoddard

THE GOPHER STATE

Anoka calls itself the HALLOWEEN Capital of the World. Over 100 years ago, the town started their spooky Halloween celebrations to stop holiday pranksters after cows were found roaming the city jail!

Tour the cured meats exhibit at the SPAM Museum in Austin. Did you know the famous canned lunch meat is cooked in its own can on the assembly line?

The CORN WATER TOWER in Rochester looks like a husked ear of corn and holds 50,000 gallons of water. Its corny cousin is a huge EAR OF CORN mounted atop a gazebo in Olivia.

LEFSE is a soft Norwegian flatbread made from potatoes. The Lefse Dagen celebration commemorates the world's largest lefse (70 pounds), baked in Starbuck in 1983.

Anglers take to the lakes to hook the stubborn WALLEYE. Glow-in-the-dark pearlescent eyes allow the fish to see at night or in murky water.

The ugly, slimy EELPOUT (think of a mash-up of a catfish and an eel) lives on the bottom of cold Minnesota lakes.

Compete in RHUBARB GOLF (using a stalk instead of a club) and the RHUBARB STALK THROW at the Rhubarb Festival in Lanesboro.

Like shopping? Then head to Minnesota! The Mall of America in Bloomington is one of the largest shopping malls in the U.S., with more than 500 stores and 50 restaurants, plus an indoor theme park. The enormous mall is the size of 78 football fields, and over 40 million people visit every year—that's more than the population of Canada! And if shopping's not your thing, Minnesota has plenty of waterways to canoe or kayak, wilderness trails to hike, and majestic waterfalls to admire.

LAKE ITASCA is the main source of the Mississippi River.

Minnesota raises the most TURKEYS in the nation. Only tom (male) turkeys "gobble." Hens (females) "click."

MINNESOTA
The North Star State

Saint Paul Winter Carnival started in 1886 and is the OLDEST WINTER CARNIVAL in the U.S. Zoom down the 300-foot-long snow slide!

GRAY TREE FROGS have the ability to partially freeze during the frigid Minnesota winters then thaw out when the weather turns warm.

The state's remote NORTHWEST ANGLE is the northernmost spot in the continental U.S. "The Angle" is only reachable by boating across Lake of the Woods or driving into Canada.

The juicy HONEYCRISP APPLE was developed at the University of Minnesota.

In Minnesota, the game "Duck, Duck, Goose" is called DUCK, DUCK, GRAY DUCK.

Gnome statues are plentiful throughout Dawson, which calls itself GNOMETOWN, USA.

Discover around 5,000 ancient Native ROCK CARVINGS, with drawings of turtles, horses, thunderbirds, and humans at Jeffers Petroglyphs in Comfrey. Tribal groups, including the Dakota, Ioway, and Cheyenne, honor the site as a sacred space.

State Favorites   COOKIE chocolate chip • VEGETABLE winter squash • SNACK Juicy (or Jucy) Lucy burger

Mississippi is the birthplace of Elvis Presley, Jimmy Buffett, Charley Pride, and Britney Spears, but no musical style is more associated with Mississippi than the blues. Emerging from the Mississippi Delta (the northwest section of the state), the soulful music was sung by enslaved West Africans in the cotton fields and then found its way into juke joints. Blues superstars such as Muddy Waters, John Lee Hooker, Robert Johnson, and B.B. King are celebrated at The Delta Blues Museum in Clarksdale.

Kool-Aid pickles, or KOOLICKLES, started in the Mississippi Delta. Pickles take a week-long Kool-Aid bath in the fridge to get their eye-popping color.

The MISSISSIPPI SANDHILL CRANE has a wingspan of more than seven feet. Only about 150 of these critically endangered cranes remain in the wild.

MISSISSIPPI

The Magnolia State

Mississippi State University set the world record for the most people (5,748) ringing COWBELLS simultaneously in 2015.

Visit the SLUGBURGER Festival in Corinth! No, they're not serving slimy creatures on a bun. A slugburger is a patty of beef or pork mixed with soybean grits that's fried golden brown. The Depression-era burgers sold for only 5¢, and back then nickels were called "slugs."

The world record for the most people eating WATERMELON at a contest (745 competitors) was set at the Watermelon Carnival in Water Valley.

As a child, Kosciusko-born OPRAH WINFREY liked to pretend-interview the crows outside her grandmother's house. Today she's a billionaire media executive!

RIVERBOATS powered by a large paddle wheel cruise up and down the mighty Mississippi River.

Go green at the "birthplace" of KERMIT THE FROG exhibit in Leland, where Muppets creator Jim Henson grew up.

NATCHEZ TRACE PARKWAY is an ancient trail from the Natchez tribe's home to hunting grounds in Tennessee.

State Favorites
SNACK cheddar cheese straws · FRUIT blueberry · SOFT DRINK Barq's root beer

The extinct JACKSON VOLCANO is buried 2,900 feet underneath the Mississippi Coliseum. The volcano hasn't erupted in over 65 million years and isn't expected to erupt again.

Mississippi produces the most farm-raised CATFISH in the country. Try fried catfish at the World Catfish Festival in Belzoni.

The nation's longest human-made BEACH (26 miles) spans from Biloxi to Henderson Point.

Wacky WATER TOWERS! Minter City painted their water tower to look like a cotton boll, while Greenville attached an actual Air Force training jet to theirs. Ruleville has two water towers: one labeled "hot" and one "cold."

The Biloxi Blessing of the Fleet Festival marks the beginning of SHRIMP-fishing season.

People line up in Jackson for the Big Apple Inn's famous PIG EAR SANDWICH.

The EGG BOWL is the football game between the Ole Miss (University of Mississippi) Rebels and the Mississippi State Bulldogs. The trophy resembles a golden egg.

Natchez is known as the BISCUIT Capital of the World.

The MISSISSIPPI CIVIL RIGHTS MUSEUM in Jackson shares stories of the struggle for equality, including those of Medgar Evers and Emmett Till.

FAST FACTS

CAPITAL Jackson

FUNNY PLACE NAMES Alligator, Arm, Basic, Hard Cash, Hot Coffee, Mhoon Landing, Possumneck, Rolling Fork, Soso, Whynot

STATE SLANG
• "FIXIN' TO" means you're going to do something.

• "I've known her since she was KNEE-HIGH TO A GRASSHOPPER," means since she was a little kid.

The **STATE QUARTER** features the state flower, the **MAGNOLIA**. Magnolia flowers can be pink, white, red, purple, or yellow and are pollinated by beetles.

FANTASTIC FOODS
• **MISSISSIPPI MUD PIE** is an intensely chocolate sheet cake covered with marshmallow crème, pecans, and fudge frosting.

• Tangy **COMEBACK SAUCE** is made with mayonnaise, ketchup, and chili sauce. It's used on fish, French fries, and even salads.

• **HOT TAMALES** in the Mississippi Delta are smaller and narrower than Mexican tamales. The corn husks are stuffed with pork or ground beef.

COOL INVENTIONS
• President Theodore "Teddy" Roosevelt's refusal to shoot a captured bear in Sharkey County in 1902 led to the creation of the **TEDDY BEAR**.

• The concept of selling **PAIRS OF SHOES IN BOXES** began in Vicksburg at Phil Gilbert's Shoe Parlor in 1884.

BOOKS *Roll of Thunder, Hear My Cry* by Mildred D. Taylor • *Glory Be* by Augusta Scattergood

FAST FACTS

CAPITAL Jefferson City

FUNNY PLACE NAMES Bacon, Blue Eye, Braggadocio, Butts, Frankenstein, Frisbee, Goodnight, Humansville, Peculiar, Sleeper, Tightwad, Turtle

STATE SLANG

MIZZOU is the University of Missouri.

T-RAVS (toasted raviolis) are breaded, deep-fried, meat-in-the-middle raviolis served with a side of marinara sauce.

The **STATE QUARTER** features LEWIS AND CLARK's return to St. Louis on the Missouri River in 1806, after their exploration of the Louisiana Purchase. Rowing the boat is YORK, Clark's enslaved servant, who did a lot of the crucial work on the expedition. The GATEWAY ARCH, often called the "Gateway to the West," is in the background.

FANTASTIC FOODS

GOOEY BUTTER CAKE is a St. Louis tradition. Legend has it that in the 1930s, a baker added too much butter to his cake batter. It was a hit anyway!

The GERBER is a toasted open-faced sandwich on long garlic-bread made with ham and PROVEL cheese (a blend of cheddar, Swiss, and provolone also used on St. Louis-style pizza).

COOL INVENTIONS

Bob Chandler created the first MONSTER TRUCK in the mid-1970s. After he videotaped "Bigfoot" (his Ford with 48-inch tires) crushing two cars in 1981, Monster Jam was born.

The ICE CREAM CONE was introduced at the 1904 St. Louis World's Fair. Legend says an ice-cream vendor ran out of cups, and Ernest A. Hamwi, a Syrian vendor of waffle-like cookies, came to the rescue with rolled-up waffles to hold the ice cream.

BOOKS *I Survived the Joplin Tornado, 2011* by Lauren Tarshis   *The Seven Wonders of Sassafras Springs* by Betty G. Birney

Take on the identity of a passenger or crew member at the TITANIC Museum Attraction in Branson and discover if you survive the sinking of the huge ocean liner.

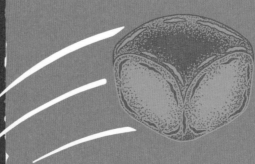

At Lambert's Cafe—the "Home of THROWED ROLLS"—the servers throw hot dinner rolls to the customers.

Charles Grigg created 7UP in St. Louis in 1929. It was originally called "Bib-Label Lithiated Lemon-Lime Soda," but funnily enough, no one could remember that name.

SLICED BREAD was first offered for sale in Chillicothe in 1928. July 7th is officially "Sliced Bread Day" in Missouri.

Gather your friends for a FLOAT TRIP down a slow-moving river atop a tube, raft, kayak, or canoe.

The southeastern part of the state is called the BOOT HEEL, because it looks like (yep, you guessed it) a boot heel!

The PIGS ALOFT MUSEUM in Linn has the country's largest collection of piggy items.

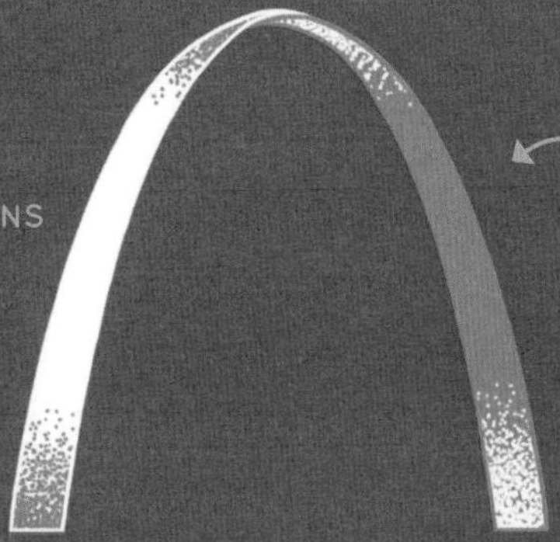

Kansas City has the most FOUNTAINS in the country.

The GATEWAY ARCH is the tallest monument in the U.S. (630 feet).

The official state animal is the MULE. A mule has a donkey father and a horse mother.

Every year, grilling teams from across the globe arrive in Kansas City (KC), Missouri, to compete in the American Royal BBQ, one of the world's biggest open barbecue competitions. KC calls itself "Barbecue Capital of the World," and "burnt ends," the crispy, flavorful end pieces of smoked beef brisket, are a hometown favorite. Also taking part in the state's hickory-smoked barbecue mania, St. Louis reportedly consumes more tangy barbecue sauce than any other U.S. city!

MISSOURI
The Show Me State

On Halloween in St. Louis, kids trick-or-treating must TELL A JOKE in order to receive candy.

Leila's HAIR MUSEUM in Independence displays wreaths made from human hair.

Checkmate! The world's largest CHESS PIECE, a 20-foot king, sits outside the World Chess Hall of Fame in St. Louis.

National COOKIE CUTTER Historical Museum in Joplin has thousands of different cookie cutters.

Up to 100,000 WILD GEESE make yearly migration pit stops on Sumner's lakes. Nearby is MAXIE, the world's largest goose statue (40 feet tall)!

Warrensburg is home to a statue of CANINE LEGEND OLD DRUM, inspiration for the phrase that dogs are "man's best friend."

MAXIE

State Favorites

DOUGHNUT cinnamon twist · DRINK Vess soda · BREAKFAST the slinger

The American COMPUTER and ROBOTICS Museum in Bozeman traces the history of the Information Age from the first written word to quantum computing.

The largest SNOWFLAKE documented was found in Fort Keogh during an 1887 storm. It measured 15 inches wide and 8 inches thick!

Floyd "Creeky" Creekmore, a former Montana rancher, held the record for world's oldest performing CLOWN until his death at age 98 in 2014.

Montana's natural beauty is supersized—wide open plains, huge mountains, spectacular rivers, and endless blue sky. Giant Springs is one of the largest freshwater springs in the nation, and the Gallatin, Madison, and Yellowstone Rivers teem with a bounty of trout, making Montana one of the best fly-fishing destinations. With more different species of mammals than any other state, Montana's elk, deer, and antelope populations easily outnumber the state's human residents.

MONTANA
THE TREASURE STATE

The smallest carnivore in North America, the LEAST WEASEL, lives in Montana.

Every spring, thousands of WHITE PELICANS with wingspans of up to nine feet migrate from the Gulf of Mexico and southern California to five locations throughout Montana to breed.

The BUCKING HORSE SALE in Miles City is all about bucking broncos, bull riding, and wild horse racing.

The LONGEST RURAL MAIL DELIVERY route is in Sidney. The carrier travels 190.7 miles daily.

The Pekin Noodle Parlor in Butte is the oldest known continuously operating CHINESE RESTAURANT in the U.S. (opened in 1911). Chinese immigrants settled in Montana in the late 1800s to work in the gold mines.

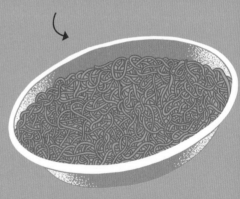

The BLEU HORSES—39 steel horse statues perched on a hillside just north of Three Forks—look very much like real horses from a distance.

Montana is the only state with a TRIPLE DIVIDE. The waters from Triple Divide Peak in Glacier National Park flow into three oceans—the Arctic, Atlantic, and Pacific.

STATE   SNACK beef jerky · SANDWICH pork chop · FRUIT huckleberry

Big Sky Country

The first LUGE RUN in North America was built by University of Montana students at Lolo Hot Springs in 1965.

The Roe River (about 201 feet in length) is one of the world's SHORTEST RIVERS (along with the D River in Lincoln City, Oregon).

Glacier National Park has around 25 active GLACIERS. In 1850, there were 80 glaciers. Based on current rates of climate change, many scientists predict all the glaciers may melt in the next few decades.

BRRRRR! Take the PENGUIN PLUNGE (a hole is cut into frozen Whitefish Lake for swimming) at the Whitefish Winter Carnival.

The fair site at the Crow Fair Celebration Powwow & Rodeo held by the Apsáalooke people of the Crow Nation is called the TIPI Capital of the World, because thousands of tipis dot the grounds.

North America's first identified dinosaur remains were unearthed in Montana in 1854. One of the largest collections of T. REX and TRICERATOPS specimens can be viewed at Museum of the Rockies in Bozeman.

The rugged Pryor Mountains are home to free-roaming bands of WILD HORSES.

FAST FACTS

CAPITAL Helena

FUNNY PLACE NAMES Anaconda, Bear Dance, Big Arm, Happy's Inn, Hungry Horse, Otter, Square Butte, Two Dot

STATE SLANG
• If something is **"TOO SPENDY,"** it's too expensive. **"A BUCK NINETY-EIGHT"** means the same.

• A **BARROW PIT** is a ditch.

• **PRAIRIE MAGGOTS** is a nickname for sheep.

The **STATE QUARTER** features a **BISON SKULL**, mountains, the Missouri River, and the words "Big Sky Country." The bison skull is a symbol of the state's rich Native culture.

FANTASTIC FOODS
• **BISON BURGERS** are made from bison meat. Bison are North America's largest land mammals, with the bulls weighing up to 2,000 pounds. See them roam at the National Bison Range near Moiese.

• Huge **CINNAMON ROLLS** the size of saucers are covered in sweet icing.

COOL INVENTIONS
• The **PORTABLE HEART MONITOR** was invented in Helena in the late 1940s by biophysicist Norman Holter. The Holter monitor can record the heart's electrical activity while a patient is away from the doctor's office.

BOOKS *Max the Mighty* by Rodman Philbrick • *Hattie Big Sky* by Kirby Larson

NEBRASKA

The Cornhusker State

What's poppin' in Nebraska? POPCORN! Nebraska is the top popcorn-producer in the nation. Here are some a-maize-ing facts: Americans eat around 17 billion quarts of popcorn every year (this would fill the Empire State Building 18 times!) and popped popcorn comes in two shapes: butterfly and mushroom. The state's longest-running annual festival is North Loup Popcorn Days, and the University of Nebraska football team is called the Cornhuskers.

Roll on down to the National Museum of ROLLER SKATING in Lincoln—it's wheely good!

The largest INDOOR RAINFOREST in the U.S. is at the Henry Doorly Zoo in Omaha.

Where's the beef? In Nebraska! The state has MORE CATTLE THAN PEOPLE. It's no wonder steak is on so many menus.

At the Leon Myers Stamp Center in Omaha, the world's largest BALL OF STAMPS was made from 4,655,000 discontinued stamps and weighs 600 pounds.

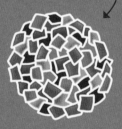

The 39 old cars at CARHENGE in Alliance are arranged exactly the same as Stonehenge, the circle of ancient stones in England.

Lee's Legendary Marbles and Collectibles in York is home to around 1 million MARBLES of every different color.

In 1872, J. Sterling Morton proposed a holiday to encourage people to plant trees for shade and windbreak on Nebraska's flat plains. He even gave out prizes for the most trees properly planted! ARBOR DAY is still celebrated on the last Friday in April.

Nicknamed "Archie," the world's largest COLUMBIAN MAMMOTH FOSSIL is on display at the University of Nebraska State Museum. It stands 14 feet tall.

State Favorites   ICE CREAM FLAVOR butter brickle · VEGETABLE corn · PIZZA TOPPING pineapple

FAST FACTS

CAPITAL Lincoln

FUNNY PLACE NAMES Bee, Boys Town, Broken Bow, Crab Orchard, Friend, Funk, Hazard, Mascot, McCool Junction, Surprise, Valentine, Wahoo, Weeping Water, Worms, Wynot

STATE SLANG
• A name seen on many buildings—**AKSARBEN**—is Nebraska spelled backward!

The **STATE QUARTER** features a covered wagon carrying pioneers with **CHIMNEY ROCK** in the background. Stretching 300 feet into the sky, Chimney Rock served as a landmark for travelers heading west on the Oregon, Mormon, and California Trails.

FANTASTIC FOODS
• Legend has it the **REUBEN SANDWICH** was invented in 1925 by Omaha grocer Reuben Kulakofsky to feed players in a late-night poker game at the Blackstone Hotel. He piled corned beef, Swiss cheese, Russian dressing, and sauerkraut on rye bread and grilled it. March 14th is Reuben Sandwich Day in Omaha.

• **RUNZAS** (also called **BIEROCKS**)—a yeasted bread pocket stuffed with beef, cabbage or sauerkraut, onions, and seasonings—were brought to Nebraska by German immigrants.

• **CHEESE FRENCHEES** are deep-fried grilled cheese sandwiches.

COOL INVENTIONS
• In 1927, the powdered drink mix **KOOL-AID** was invented in Hastings, when Edwin Perkins transformed his soft drink syrup "Fruit Smack" into powder to make it easier to ship. Kool-Aid is the official state drink.

• Made in Duncan, orange-colored **DOROTHY LYNCH DRESSING** is used by Nebraskans on salads, as a dip, and as a sandwich topping.

BOOKS *The Girl Who Circumnavigated Fairyland in a Ship of Her Own Making* by Catherynne M. Valente
• *Room One: A Mystery or Two* by Andrew Clements

Catch a flying hot dog! DER VIENER SCHLINGER is a pressurized cannon that launches hot dogs into the stands during University of Nebraska Husker football games.

The world's largest COVERED PORCH SWING in Hebron sits about 18 adults or 24 children.

The Pilgrim Holiness Church in Arthur was BUILT FROM HAY BALES (covered with plaster and stucco).

The WAYNE CHICKEN SHOW festival celebrates the clucking bird with an egg toss, a hardboiled egg eating contest, and a chicken dance.

Nebraska is the only state with a UNICAMERAL (single-chamber) legislative government. It was also the first state to have two women run against each other for governor.

OPEN 2025

The world's largest TIME CAPSULE in Seward was sealed for 50 years in 1975. The vault is topped by a concrete pyramid and inside are over 5,000 items, including a motorcycle and two cars.

While Nevada (pronounce it "Nev-ADD-ah"—not "Nev-AH-dah") has hundreds of snow-capped mountain ranges, it's often best known for its sun-baked desert and the shining city of Las Vegas. Nevada's the driest state, with less than 10 inches of rain per year. Visitors love the dry desert heat combined with the fabulous shows and casinos, making tourism the state's top industry.

Soar 550 feet above the Las Vegas Strip on the High Roller, the nation's tallest FERRIS WHEEL.

Play a vintage machine at the PINBALL Hall of Fame in Las Vegas.

SEVEN MAGIC MOUNTAINS, the 30-foot stacks of brightly colored boulders in the Mojave Desert, is an exhibit by Swiss artist Ugo Rondinone.

THE SILVER STATE

NEVADA

The morbid, the merrier! Coffin It Up, a custom coffin-making business in Pahrump offers tours of their COFFINS, hearses, and coffin cemetery.

At the National COWBOY POETRY Gathering in Elko, ranchers and cowboys share poems about their lives.

The bronze TOILET PAPER HERO statue in Boulder City honors a "sanitation engineer" who cleaned outhouses during the construction of the Hoover Dam.

The nation's largest CHOCOLATE FOUNTAIN at the Bellagio Hotel in Las Vegas is 27 feet tall!

Twelve spooky GHOSTS haunt the Mojave Desert near the ghost town of Rhyolite. Polish-Belgian artist Albert Szukalski created THE LAST SUPPER sculpture to echo Leonardo da Vinci's famous painting of the same name.

OPEN

The NEON Museum in Las Vegas shines bright with over 250 historic neon signs.

State Favorites   ICE CREAM FLAVOR rocky road · BREAKFAST steak and eggs · VEGETABLE onions

The Clown Motel in Tonopah is decorated in CLOWNS and boasts what may be the largest private collection of clown figurines.

The EXTRATERRESTRIAL HIGHWAY is a deserted stretch of road between Alamo and Rachel. Many people claim to have spotted aliens and UFOs around here.

MOOOO! Alfie the "BIG BOVINE OF THE DESERT" welcomes visitors in Amargosa Valley.

AIR RACING is called "the world's fastest motor sport." At the STIHL National Championship Air Races in Reno, planes zoom over 500 miles per hour!

The "Spirit Cave Mummy"—the OLDEST HUMAN SKELETON (10,600 years old) found in the U.S.—was discovered in a small cave in northern Nevada's Great Basin Desert.

"DIED EATING LIBRARY PASTE" is a tombstone epitaph at the Goldfield Pioneer Cemetery.

RiP
DIED EATING LIBRARY PASTE

Learn about MONSTER MOVIE special-effects makeup and props at Tom Devlin's Monster Museum in Boulder City.

FAST FACTS

CAPITAL Carson City

FUNNY PLACE NAMES Carp, Dinner Station, Duckwater, Jackpot, Jiggs, Lovelock, Searchlight, Stagecoach, Steamboat

STATE SLANG
_____ is the four-mile stretch of neon lights, hotels, and casinos in Las Vegas.

_____ is a frozen fog that forms in the northern Nevada mountain valleys.

The **STATE QUARTER** features three _____ and _____, the state flower. Nevada is home to most of the nation's wild horses and burros.

FANTASTIC FOODS
_____ is a popular appetizer of cooked and chilled shrimp served in a parfait glass with a lemon wedge and cocktail sauce (a mixture of ketchup, Tabasco, and Worcestershire). Some reports have Las Vegas serving 60,000 pounds of shrimp a day!

_____ is a thick steak cooked between two thinner steaks to give the thick steak a perfectly rare center. The Basque people, who come from an area between France and Spain, settled in Nevada during the gold rush and many became sheep herders. The National Basque Festival is held every year in Elko.

COOL INVENTIONS
Jacob Davis, a tailor from Reno, added rivets to pants to make them tougher for miners. He teamed up with Levi Strauss to invent the first pair of _____ in 1873.

BOOKS Mustang: _Wild Spirit of the West_ by Marguerite Henry   _Moon Shadow_ by Chris Platt

FAST FACTS

CAPITAL Concord

FUNNY PLACE NAMES Bath, Bear Notch, Breakfast Hill, Center Sandwich, Dummer, Freedom, Happy Corner, Horse Corner

STATE SLANG:

• A **FLATLANDER** is anyone from south of New Hampshire who visits to **LEAF-PEEP** (look at the brilliant fall foliage) or see the covered bridges.

• A **DRAW** is where you keep your socks and undies. New Hampshire folks often drop the "-er" sound at the ends of words.

The **STATE QUARTER** features what was once the state's most famous natural rock formation, the **OLD MAN OF THE MOUNTAIN**, which looked like a man's profile. It collapsed in 2003.

FANTASTIC FOODS

• With so many fresh lakes, **FRIED LAKE BASS** is a state favorite. The flaky, white fish is filleted, then fried.

• The **STEAK BOMB** is similar to Philadelphia's cheesesteak. These submarine sandwiches have shaved steak, melted cheese, salami, sautéed bell peppers, onions, and mushrooms.

• A French-Canadian dish, **POUTINE** is French fries, brown gravy, and cheese curds. In the late 1800s and early 1900s, many French-Canadians moved to New Hampshire to work in the textile mills.

COOL INVENTIONS

• The first American **ALARM CLOCK** was created in 1787 by Levi Hutchins of Concord. The alarm wasn't adjustable—it only rang at 4:00 a.m. (which was when HE wanted to wake up!).

BOOKS *Half A Chance* by Cynthia Lord • *A Gathering of Days: A New England Girl's Journal, 1830–1832* by Joan W. Blos

The Granite State

The Mount Washington Cog Railway is the world's first MOUNTAIN-CLIMBING COG RAILWAY. Every day it chugs to the summit of the highest peak in the Northeast—and one of the windiest places on Earth.

The world's first WIND FARM (giant wind turbines spin to create electricity) was installed in 1980 on the shoulder of Crotched Mountain.

The Hinsdale Post Office has been in the same building since 1816 and is the OLDEST CONTINUOUSLY OPERATING POST OFFICE in the U.S.

New Hampshire holds the FIRST PRESIDENTIAL PRIMARY in the nation.

Every October at the Goffstown GIANT PUMPKIN REGATTA, huge pumpkins are scooped out, decorated, and used as boats!

"MARY HAD A LITTLE LAMB" was written by writer and editor Sarah Josepha Hale in 1830. It may have been inspired by a student who brought a lamb to school when Hale was working as a teacher in Newport.

Wolfeboro calls itself "The OLDEST SUMMER RESORT in America." Since the 1770s, it's been a popular summer destination for New England families.

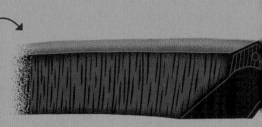

The Cornish-Windsor Bridge, the LONGEST WOODEN COVERED BRIDGE in the U.S. (about 449 feet long), is shared by New Hampshire and Vermont.

NEW HAMPSHIRE

It's apple everything in New Hampshire! Apple orchards are plentiful throughout the state, growing almost 100 varieties of the fruit. When fall arrives and the leaves turn a blazing red, orange, and yellow, roadside stands sell crisp apple cider (the state beverage) and apple cider doughnuts dusted with cinnamon-sugar. Cut an apple in half (across the core) and you'll see a star shape!

New Hampshire has more SNOWMOBILE trails (around 7,000 miles!) than highways.

Many CARNIVOROUS PLANTS grow in the state's bogs. Sundews, pitcher plants, and bladderworts devour their insect or microscopic aquatic prey.

Funspot at Weirs Beach is the world's largest GAMES ARCADE.

How sweet! Chutters candy store in Littleton boasts the world's LONGEST CANDY COUNTER—112 feet of glass candy-filled jars!

In October at the NH Grass Drags and Watercross in Fremont, the fastest SNOWMOBILE RACERS compete not on snow but on grass and on water. Snowmobiling on water is also known as WATER SKIPPING.

Every year, the Keene Pumpkin Festival tries to set a new record for the number of JACK-O'-LANTERNS lit at one event. In 2013, they reached 30,581.

The world's largest FAIRY HOUSE TOUR is in Portsmouth. The tiny houses made out of natural materials are perfect for fairy visitors.

At a cemetery in Washington, there's a GRAVESTONE FOR AN AMPUTATED LEG that belonged to Captain Samuel Jones Jr. In 1804, he had an accident while moving a house, causing his leg to be surgically removed (probably without anesthesia to dull the pain!) and he buried it.

State Favorites   COOKIE pumpkin spice · BREAKFAST pancakes with maple syrup · DESSERT Grape-Nut pudding

LUCY THE ELEPHANT stands 65 feet tall in Margate City. Built in 1881, visitors can climb the spiral staircase inside her belly to the top.

New Jersey is the only state where you're not allowed to PUMP YOUR OWN GAS.

Pass GO! The street names in the game Monopoly come from ATLANTIC CITY, which also has the longest boardwalk in the world. And SALT WATER TAFFY was created in Atlantic City in 1883.

Kingda Ka at Six Flags Great Adventure in Jackson is the TALLEST AND FASTEST ROLLER COASTER in the nation with a top speed of 128 miles per hour.

New Jersey has more HORSES per square mile than any other state. The United States Equestrian Team is based in Gladstone.

FAST FACTS

CAPITAL Trenton

FUNNY PLACE NAMES Brick, Buttzville, Cheesequake, Egg Harbor City, Hi-Nella, Rudeville, Ship Bottom, Wall

STATE SLANG
• "YOUSE GUYS GOIN' DOWN THE SHORE?" means "Are you all going to the beach?"

• MISCHIEF NIGHT is the night before Halloween, when kids pull pranks.

The **STATE QUARTER** features General George Washington leading his troops across the Delaware River to Trenton to fight the British. During the REVOLUTIONARY WAR, more battles were fought in New Jersey than any other state.

FANTASTIC FOODS
• TAYLOR HAM (also called pork roll), served on a hard roll with egg and cheese, is a popular breakfast and lunch.

• Italian-Americans created CHICKEN PARMIGIANA ("Chicken Parm")—breaded chicken cutlets baked with marinara sauce and melted mozzarella cheese.

• In the Garden State, a SLOPPY JOE is a triple-decker rye bread sandwich made with deli meats along with Swiss cheese, coleslaw, and Russian dressing.

COOL INVENTIONS
• Josephine Dickson was always cutting her fingers while cooking, and she needed help to wrap them in the bulky bandages of the time. So, in 1920, her husband Earle attached a small piece of folded gauze to a strip of surgical tape and invented the BAND-AID. Johnson & Johnson in New Brunswick manufactured it.

• The first DRIVE-IN MOVIE THEATER was in Camden in 1933.

• Les Paul of Mahwah invented the SOLID-BODY ELECTRIC GUITAR in 1941.

BOOKS *The Serpent's Secret* by Sayantani DasGupta • *The Hoboken Chicken Emergency* by Daniel Pinkwater

UNIO

The world's TALLEST WATER SPHERE (212 feet) is in Union.

The College of New Jersey (now Princeton University) and Rutgers University played what's thought to be the first COLLEGE FOOTBALL GAME on November 6th, 1869.

Ocean City is home to a WEATHER PREDICTING HERMIT CRAB. If Martin Z. Mollusk sees his shadow, it means summer will come early.

The BABY RUTH candy bar was named after President Grover Cleveland's daughter Ruth. Cleveland is the only U.S. president born in New Jersey.

CHEERLEADING was started in Princeton University in 1869. In the early days, it was an all-male sport.

The JERSEY DEVIL— a legendary creature with a goat-like head, bat wings, cloven hooves, and a forked tail—supposedly lives in the forested Pine Barrens.

Oak Tree Road in Edison and neighboring Iselin is often called LITTLE INDIA, and among its South Asian groceries and sari stores are around 60 Indian and Pakistani restaurants.

NEW JERSEY

THE GARDEN STATE

Diners are a "Jersey thing." With over 500 across the state, New Jersey is called the "Diner Capital of the World." After entering past a revolving cake display, patrons slide into well-worn booths and scan voluminous menus. Anything and everything is served at a NJ diner—at any time of the day or night. Highlights of a true diner experience include disco fries (French fries topped with mozzarella cheese and brown gravy), Greek gyros, and breakfast (especially for dinner!).

Made from intricate hand-carved marble, BAPS Shri Swaminarayan Mandir in Robbinsville is the nation's largest HINDU TEMPLE (162-acre complex).

Northlandz, called the world's largest MINIATURE WONDERLAND, features 100 miniature trains traveling on 8 miles of track.

NEW YORK

NEW JERSEY

The first UNDERWATER TUNNEL FOR CARS—the Holland Tunnel—was built in 1927 to connect New Jersey and New York.

By the time of his death in 1931, THOMAS EDISON held 1,093 patents including the light bulb, phonograph, and early movie camera (kinetograph). Edison's Menlo Park laboratory was the world's first research and development facility.

State Favorites   SANDWICH Taylor ham, egg, and cheese · FRUIT Jersey tomatoes · CANDY salt water taffy

New Mexico is the only state with an official state question: "Red or green?" This means "Do you want red or green chile sauce with your enchilada, cheeseburger, apple pie (or, really, anything on your plate)?" Order "Christmas," and you'll get red and green chiles together. New Mexico grows more pounds of chile peppers than any other state. Every year, the town of Hatch (known as the Chile Capital of the World) spices things up with an eye-watering chile-eating contest. How many can you eat?

Land of Enchantment

Santa Fe is the OLDEST CAPITAL CITY in North America. It was founded in 1610, a decade before the Pilgrims landed at Plymouth. Santa Fe is also the HIGHEST STATE CAPITAL (7,199 feet above sea level).

One of the longest RISTRAS (over 157 feet) was braided at the New Mexico State Fair in 2008. Ristras—strings of dried chile peppers—are said to bring good luck and health.

NEW MEXICO

Hundreds of colorful HOT AIR BALLOONS fill the skies at the Albuquerque International Balloon Fiesta, the world's largest ballooning event.

Anthony (a tiny town straddling the New Mexico-Texas border) is known as the LEAP YEAR Capital of the World. Every four years, it throws a big birthday party for people born on February 29th.

A mysterious object crashed near Roswell in 1947—was it sent by aliens? Learn all about UNIDENTIFIED FLYING OBJECTS at the International UFO Museum and Research Center. Or enter your dog in the ALIEN PET COSTUME Contest at the Roswell UFO Festival.

ZOZOBRA or "Old Man Gloom" is a giant marionette that's lit on fire in Santa Fe every September to "extinguish" the sadness from the prior year.

Up to 500,000 bats live in the CARLSBAD CAVERNS. Every evening, they swarm out of the caves at 28 minutes past sunset.

State Favorites

CANDY piñon nut brittle · VEGETABLE frijoles (pinto beans) · SNACK frito pie

Spaceport America is the first purpose-built commercial SPACEPORT in the world. In 2023, Virgin Galactic took its first tourists to the edge of space from this desert tarmac. Want to go? A ticket costs $450,000!

FLIGT Nº 71
DESTINATION SATURN

The Gathering of Nations is the largest POWWOW in North America with over 565 U.S. and 220 Canadian Indigenous tribes traveling to Albuquerque to celebrate their cultural heritage.

TURQUOISE is an opaque blue-to-green mineral first mined by the Ancestral Pueblo people. After turquoise is mined, layers of rock and dirt are removed then it's shaped and polished to be used in jewelry.

The GREATER ROADRUNNER, the state bird, has big feet with four toes—two pointing forward and two pointing backward—that make X-shaped footprints.

In TAOS PUEBLO, the Tiwa-speaking tribe of the Pueblo Nation have lived continuously in multi-story adobe villages that are more than 1,000 years old. They climbed long, wooden ladders to enter through square holes in the roof instead of a front door. The ladders were taken away in times of danger.

Birders flock to the Festival of the Cranes to celebrate the winter migration of SANDHILL CRANES to the Bosque del Apache National Wildlife Refuge.

FAST FACTS

CAPITAL Santa Fe

FUNNY PLACE NAMES Bread Springs, Candy Kitchen, Dusty, Elephant Butte, Mosquero ("Swarm of Flies"), Pep, Pie Town, Queen, Raton ("Rat" or "Mouse"), Sunshine, Tijeras ("Scissors"), Truth or Consequences

STATE SLANG
• During the winter holidays, New Mexicans place candles in little paper bags filled with sand to festively light paths. In the southern part of the state they're called LUMINARIAS, but up north they're FAROLITOS.

The STATE QUARTER features an outline of the state's map with the ZIA SUN SYMBOL on the state capital, Santa Fe. Both the sun and the number four are sacred to the Zia Pueblo tribe.

FANTASTIC FOODS
• POSOLE stew is a traditional celebration dish. Hominy (giant dried white corn kernels) are simmered for hours along with chiles, onions, and pork.

• BIZCOCHITO are crispy butter cookies flavored with cinnamon and anise.

• SOPAIPILLAS are pillow-shaped, fried tortilla dough served sweet or savory. For dessert, they're drizzled with honey or anise syrup and covered with powdered sugar.

COOL INVENTIONS
• Tia Sophia's restaurant in Santa Fe claims to be the first in 1975 to put the BREAKFAST BURRITO on a menu. A breakfast burrito is eggs, cheese, potatoes, and often meat wrapped in a warm flour tortilla and smothered with chile sauce.

BOOKS *Tortilla Sun* by Jennifer Cervantes • *. . . And Now Miguel* by Joseph Krumgold

It's against state law to take a SELFIE WITH A TIGER.

Every July 4th, Nathan's in Coney Island holds its famous HOT DOG EATING CONTEST.

In the center of a pond in Oneida, Cross Island Chapel is the world's SMALLEST CHURCH. It seats only two people!

Hartsdale Pet Cemetery is the world's OLDEST OPERATING PET CEMETERY, with over 80,000 dogs, cats, horses, birds, primates, and even a lion that lived at the Plaza Hotel in NYC.

ALBERT EINSTEIN'S EYEBALLS are stored in a safe deposit box in NYC.

RIP SNUFFLES

The NATIONAL TOY HALL OF FAME in Rochester displays the best toys ever made.

FAST FACTS

CAPITAL Albany

FUNNY PLACE NAMES Big Moose, Butternuts, Dadville, Fishkill, Handsome Eddy, Horseheads, Neversink, Truthville, West Almond

STATE SLANG
• A **SLICE** means a piece of pizza. A **PLAIN PIE** is a cheese pizza.

• **THE CITY** refers to Manhattan. **UPSTATE** is everything north of NYC.

The **STATE QUARTER** features the

STATUE OF LIBERTY in NYC's harbor, which has welcomed immigrants to the U.S. since 1886.

FANTASTIC FOODS
• Jewish immigrants from Poland introduced **BAGEL AND LOX**

(smoked salmon) and **PASTRAMI ON RYE** with mustard to NYC.

• **BEEF ON WECK**—a popular sandwich in Buffalo—is roast beef with grated horseradish on a kummelweck roll.

COOL INVENTIONS
• **TOILET PAPER** was invented in NYC in 1857 by Joseph Gayetty. Before this, most people wiped with catalogues!

• Marie Van Brittan Brown invented the first **HOME SECURITY SYSTEM** in 1966 for her own house in Queens. Her original design contained a camera, two-way microphone, peepholes, monitors, and an alarm button to contact the police.

BOOKS *From the Mixed-Up Files of Mrs. Basil E. Frankweiler* by E.L. Konigsburg • *New Kid* by Jerry Craft

Blocks of ice from Lake Flower are stacked to form an enormous ICE PALACE at the Saranac Lake Winter Carnival.

Ride a SQUARE-WHEELED TRICYCLE at the National Museum of Mathematics in Manhattan!

Take a spin on one of six antique MERRY-GO-ROUNDS in Binghamton, which calls itself the Carousel Capital of the World.

NEW YORK

New York has . . . a lot. There's a lot of apple orchards (growing enough apples each year to bake 500 million apple pies) and a lot of dairy farms (producing the most yogurt in the nation and more Greek yogurt than Greece). There's a lot of land—Adirondack Park is larger than Yellowstone National Park. New York City (NYC) has a lot of people—(more than 40 of the 50 states) and 36% of them were born in other countries, making NYC a true melting pot. The "City That Never Sleeps" also has a lot of Broadway theaters, museums, fashion designers—and billionaires (the most in the nation!).

The Empire State

Guptill's Arena in Cohoes is the world's largest INDOOR ROLLER-SKATING RINK.

At the end of summer, the West Indian American Day Carnival fills the streets of Brooklyn with sounds of CARIBBEAN CALYPSO.

One World Trade Center (The Freedom Tower) in NYC is the nation's TALLEST SKYSCRAPER at 1,776 feet.

A giant roll of Pep-O-Mint LIFE SAVERS graces Gouverneur, home town of the company's owner.

Annie Edson Taylor, a 63-year-old teacher, was the first to survive the 167-foot drop inside a barrel over NIAGARA FALLS in 1901.

Families in Saratoga Springs celebrate Christmas by smashing a candy PEPPERMINT PIG in pieces with a tiny hammer.

In 1901, New York became the first state to require LICENSE PLATES on vehicles. Each car owner got to make their own with their initials.

 State Favorites DOUGHNUT cronut • SNACK Saratoga potato chips • COOKIE black and white (half moon)

NORTH CAROLINA

The Tar Heel State

The great state debate is which barbecue style is better—Eastern or Lexington? Eastern (by the coast) roasts a whole hog and seasons it while cooking with tangy vinegar and pepper sauce ("mop sauce.") Lexington (in the mountains) roasts a pork shoulder then covers it in thick, sweet, ketchup-based sauce. North Carolinians have tried (unsuccessfully) to have one style or the other declared the official state barbecue. With no clear winner, they keep on enjoying DOUBLE BBQ!

The nation's FIRST MINIATURE GOLF COURSE was built in 1916 by James Barber in Pinehurst. Legend has it he said, "This'll do," upon seeing it finished, and named the course . . . Thistle Dhu.

The 36-foot-tall world's largest CHEST OF DRAWERS in High Point (the "Furniture Capital of the World") was constructed in 1926.

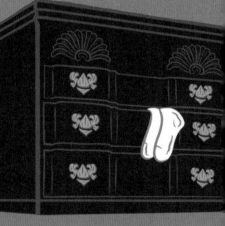

COLLARD GREENS are often eaten on New Year's Day to bring wealth, because their leaves look like folded money. Greens reign supreme at the Ayden Collard Festival.

At the UNDERWATER BICYCLE RACE near Beaufort, divers race bicycles along the starboard side of the USS *Indra*, now an artificial reef.

Taste a CHEERWINE-flavored taco at the Cheerwine Festival in Salisbury, where the "Uniquely Southern" wild-cherry soft drink was created in 1917.

The TALLEST LIGHTHOUSE in the U.S. (over 198 feet) is in Cape Hatteras.

The gnarled MOTHER VINE on Roanoke Island is about 400 years old and thought to be the oldest SCUPPERNONG GRAPE vine in North America.

The Immaculate Baking Company baked the largest COOKIE (101 feet wide and over 40,000 pounds!) in Flat Rock in 2003.

State Favorites

DRINK sweet tea · DESSERT lemon bar · VEGETABLE sweet potatoes

The FEBRUARY ONE MONUMENT in Greensboro commemorates the lunch counter sit-in on February 1st, 1960, by four brave North Carolina A&T State University students who confronted racial inequality in the South.

A metal BIG ACORN is lowered from a crane to celebrate New Year's Eve in Raleigh, known as the "City of Oaks."

GRAVEYARD OF THE ATLANTIC is a nickname for the perilous waters off the Outer Banks, site of more than 2,000 shipwrecks.

It's against state law for BINGO sessions to last longer than five hours.

Competitors in the KRISPY KREME Challenge in Raleigh run 2.5 miles, eat 12 glazed doughnuts then run another 2.5 miles in under an hour (without vomiting!). Vernon Rudolph founded Krispy Kreme in Winston-Salem in 1937.

At the WOOLLY-WORM Festival in Banner Elk, fuzzy caterpillars race for the title of official weather predictor. A woolly worm's body has 13 segments, each corresponding to a week in winter. Many farmers believe if a segment is light brown, the week will be mild. If a segment's black, the week will be very cold.

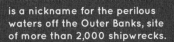

FAST FACTS

CAPITAL Raleigh

FUNNY PLACE NAMES Bald Head Island, Bat Cave, Boogertown, Frying Pan Landing, Lizard Lick, Meat Camp, Rabbit, Tick Bite, Toast, Whynot

STATE SLANG

• "BLESS YOUR HEART" has many meanings, depending on tone. It can be sincere or a sweetly disguised insult.

• YONDER is a distant location—"Take that road over yonder."

The **STATE QUARTER** features Orville and Wilbur Wright's famous FIRST AIRPLANE FLIGHT in 1903 at Kitty Hawk on North Carolina's Outer Banks.

FANTASTIC FOODS

• HUSH PUPPIES are deep-fried cornbread often served with fried seafood or barbecue. It's said that years ago, people tossed bits of fried dough to the barking dogs in the fishing villages to get them to "hush."

• MORAVIAN COOKIES are wafer-thin, spiced molasses cookies first baked by the Moravians who settled in Salem (now Winston-Salem) in the 1700s.

• DEVILED EGGS are hard-boiled eggs cut in half and stuffed with mashed yolks mixed with mayonnaise, mustard, and seasonings. Centuries ago, "deviling" meant to make a food spicy.

COOL INVENTIONS

• In 1893, Caleb Bradham created a new soft drink in his drugstore in New Bern and sold it as "Brad's Drink." Five years later, he changed the name to PEPSI-COLA.

• In 1892, North Carolina-born Sarah Boone invented the modern-day IRONING BOARD with collapsible legs and a padded cover. Before this, a plank of wood was usually placed across two chairs.

BOOKS *Three Times Lucky* by Sheila Turnage • *Wish* by Barbara O'Connor

North Dakota is so happy! It's consistently ranked as one of the happiest places to live in the U.S. About 90% of the state is farmland. North Dakota grows the most durum wheat (used for pasta) in the country —enough to make 17 billion servings of spaghetti every year! And according to the buzz, it's the nation's #1 honey producer. It's also the state with the fewest visitors—making North Dakota an excellent place to live, because there's so much untouched, natural beauty and zero crowds.

The COLORED PENCIL FENCE at Red River Zoo in Fargo is made up of over 1,000 large colored pencils.

The rare, wild NOKOTA HORSE is found in the southwestern corner of the state.

In Grand Forks, it's against the law to throw a SNOWBALL on public or private property.

NORTH DAKOTA

THE PEACE GARDEN STATE

Pass the ketchup! At Potato Bowl USA in Grand Forks, the world's largest FRENCH FRY FEED cooks up over 8,000 fries for 10,000 hungry people.

Start your engines for LAWN MOWER RACING—the mow the merrier!

Like to BLOW BUBBLES in the tub? The Mr. Bubble Museum at the Harold Schafer Heritage Center in Medora is all about bubble bath fun.

The INTERNATIONAL PEACE GARDEN on the United States/Canada border honors the strong friendship between the two nations. Inside the Peace Chapel, you can literally walk across the room and be in Canada!

The world's largest BUFFALO STATUE (but it's actually a bison!) stands in Jamestown. The 26-foot-tall, 60-ton concrete giant is named Dakota Thunder.

State Favorites   SNACK chocolate-covered potato chips • FRUIT chokecherries • COOKIE krumkake

Highway 21, called the ENCHANTED HIGHWAY, is decorated between Gladstone and Regent by some of the world's largest SCRAP METAL SCULPTURES by artist Gary Greff.

The huge W'EEL TURTLE statue in Dunseith was made from over 2,000 steel tire rims that George Gottbrecht had collected for years. Why a turtle? Dunseith is in the foothills of the Turtle Mountains.

Highway 46 stretches across 121 miles of prairie and is the LONGEST STRAIGHT ROAD in the U.S.

A 30-foot-tall DALA HORSE (a brightly painted wooden horse symbolizing Swedish folk art) stands in Scandinavian Heritage Park in Minot.

One of North Dakota's nicknames is the FLICKERTAIL STATE, after the energetic Richardson's ground squirrel, which has a tail that flicks.

SUNDOGS—often seen in North Dakota—are rainbow rings or colored spots of light that appear around the sun in cold weather. The natural phenomenon is caused by refraction of sunlight through ice crystals in the air.

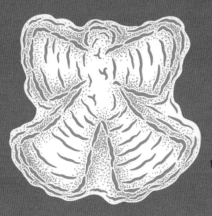

The record for the most people (8,962) making SNOW ANGELS simultaneously was set in Bismarck on February 17th, 2007.

FAST FACTS

CAPITAL Bismarck

FUNNY PLACE NAMES Buttzville, Cannon Ball, Concrete, Deep, Four Bears Village, Inkster, Pick City, Porcupine, Rugby, Starkweather, Wild Rice, Zap

STATE SLANG
• "UFF-DA!" is exclaimed when someone's surprised, baffled, shocked, or dismayed. It's a Norwegian expression, and the region's Scandinavian heritage is celebrated at Rutland's Uffda Day Fall Festival.

The STATE QUARTER features an AMERICAN BISON grazing in front of rugged buttes. Bison are often called

"buffalo," but did you know that true buffalo are found only in Asia and Africa? Early European settlers in the U.S. mistakenly believed the bison were buffalo, so messed up the name.

FANTASTIC FOODS
• KNOEPHLA, a creamy chicken and dumpling soup containing celery, carrots, and potatoes, was brought to North Dakota by German-Russian immigrants.

• CHEESE BUTTONS, or KASE KNEPFLA, are German-Russian cottage cheese and onion-filled dumplings similar to ravioli or pierogi.

• FLEISCHKUECHLE is a German-Russian fried meat pie.

COOL INVENTIONS
• CREAM OF WHEAT, the nation's first hot breakfast cereal, was invented in Grand Forks in 1893. As a way to help his flour mill make money during hard times, head miller Tom Amidon took the farina, the whitest part of the wheat, and cooked it into a hot cereal.

BOOKS *Wild Life* by Cynthia DeFelice • *Fly Away* by Patricia MacLachlan

Want good fortune? A popular Ohio superstition says you should carry a buckeye nut in your pocket. Buckeye trees, the state tree, are found throughout the Ohio River Valley. The shiny brown nut with a light tan patch in the center got its name because it resembled the eye of a male deer. Buckeyes can't be eaten (they're toxic), so instead Ohioans gobble up "buckeye candy," balls of creamy peanut butter fudge dipped in rich chocolate.

OHIO

THE BUCKEYE STATE

The ROCK & ROLL HALL OF FAME was built in Cleveland because local deejay Alan Freed popularized the phrase and promoted the first rock 'n' roll show at Cleveland Arena on March 21st, 1952.

Ohio has the only NON-RECTANGULAR STATE FLAG.

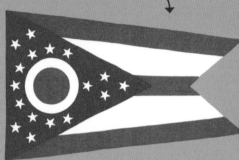

The TWINS Days Festival in Twinsburg is the largest annual gathering of twins and multiples in the world.

The world's largest OFFICE STAMP (49 feet long, 70,000 pounds), created by sculptors Claes Oldenburg and Coosje van Bruggen, makes its mark in a Cleveland park.

The country's largest number of ALPACA farms are in Ohio. Alpacas look goofy, because they have no teeth in the top-front of their mouths.

Strut the runway in an outfit crafted entirely out of DUCK TAPE at the Duck Tape Festival in Avon! The waterproof tape was invented during World War II to seal ammunition cases. It may have been called "duck tape" because it repelled water—like a duck's back.

DUCK

In 1869, the Cincinnati Red Stockings (now the Cincinnati Reds) became America's FIRST PROFESSIONAL BASEBALL CLUB.

STaTe Favorites   JUICE tomato • BREAKFAST goetta breakfast sandwich • DESSERT lemon pie

FAST FACTS

CAPITAL Columbus

FUNNY PLACE NAMES Celeryville, Dull, Fleatown, Hills and Dales, Kitchen, Knockemstiff, Mentor-on-the-Lake, Mudsock, Pee Pee, Pepper Pike, Revenge, River Styx

STATE SLANG
• The **THREE C'S** are Columbus, Cleveland, and Cincinnati—the state's three largest cities.

• Instead of "Excuse me?" Ohioans often say **"PLEASE?"** when not understanding something.

The **STATE QUARTER** features an **ASTRONAUT** and a **BIPLANE**, because astronauts Neil Armstrong and John Glenn were both born in Ohio, as were Wilbur and Orville Wright, the inventors of the first powered airplane. Dayton is home to the National Museum of the U.S. Air Force.

FANTASTIC FOODS
• **CINCINNATI CHILI** is seasoned with cinnamon and cocoa powder and served over a pile of spaghetti then topped in shredded cheese.

• Cleveland's **POLISH BOY** sandwich is kielbasa on a toasted bun, topped with French fries and coleslaw and drenched in barbecue sauce.

COOL INVENTIONS
• A **THREE-LIGHT TRAFFIC LIGHT** was invented by Garrett Morgan in 1923. He also invented an early **GAS MASK** and a **HAIR-STRAIGHTENING CREAM**.

• The card game **UNO** was created in 1971 by Milford barber Merle Robbins and his family. After arguing with his son about how to play the game Crazy Eights, Robbins decided to create his own game with his own rules!

BOOKS *Other Words for Home* by Jasmine Warga • *Out of My Mind* by Sharon M. Draper

At 30 feet long, McKinley Street in Bellefontaine may be the nation's **SMALLEST STREET**.

At the **SOAP BOX DERBY** World Championships held in Akron, the cars may use only gravity to move.

The **WASHBOARD** Music Festival in Logan celebrates Appalachian Mountain culture with foot stompin' tunes played on a washboard.

Every year on March 15th, **TURKEY VULTURES** (known locally as buzzards) return to roost in the trees of Hinckley.

Legend has it a huge **SEA MONSTER**-like creature named Bessie lives in Lake Erie.

The Troll Hole Museum in Alliance boasts the world's largest **TROLL DOLL** collection.

Sugarcreek, the "Little Switzerland of Ohio," is home to the world's largest **CUCKOO CLOCK** (23 feet tall). Ohio is also the nation's top producer of SWISS CHEESE.

Elecktro, on display at the Mansfield Memorial Museum, is the "oldest surviving American **ROBOT** in the world." Built by Westinghouse Electric Corporation in the 1930s, Elecktro could speak and move (super-cool back then!).

The PANHANDLE is a strip of land in western Oklahoma shaped like the handle of a cooking pan. The Panhandle town of Beaver hosts the WORLD COW CHIP THROWING CONTEST. A cow chip is dried cow manure (poop!).

Strum on at the American Banjo Museum in Oklahoma City, home to one of the largest BANJO collections.

The Fried Onion Burger Day Festival in El Reno cooks up the world's largest FRIED ONION BURGER, weighing over 750 pounds.

It's rumored that the thousands of ACTION FIGURES at the Toy and Action Figure Museum in Pauls Valley come alive each night!

WATERMELON is the STATE VEGETABLE; however, most botanists classify watermelon as a fruit. Go figure!

A special exhibit at the American Pigeon Museum in Oklahoma City honors the hero PIGEONS that flew hundreds of miles to deliver secret messages during the two world wars.

CAPITAL Oklahoma City

FUNNY PLACE NAMES
America, Big Cabin, Cement, Cloudy, Cookietown, Greasy, Happyland, Okay

STATE SLANG
A is a storm or tornado shelter, usually underground.

A is a wallet.

The **STATE QUARTER** features the state bird, the , which has a long, forked tail and eats insects, hence its name. The daisy-like state wildflower, the INDIAN BLANKET, covers the ground in bright colors that resemble Native blankets.

FANTASTIC FOODS
Oklahoma has an official state meal. The 12-dish menu includes CHICKEN FRIED STEAK, fried okra, cornbread, and pecan pie. Chicken fried steak doesn't have any chicken. It's a thin steak coated in flour and fried crispy (like a chicken) then ladled with white gravy.

COOL INVENTIONS
Sylvan Goldman introduced the first SHOPPING CART on wheels at Oklahoma City's Humpty Dumpty supermarket in 1937, after seeing that people couldn't fit all their groceries into a hand-held basket.

Charles Burford invented the first BREAD TWIST TIE machine in 1961 in Maysville. The color of the twist tie, or plastic tab, on a grocery store bread wrapper is a secret code showing the day of the week it was baked.

BOOKS *Where the Red Fern Grows* by Wilson Rawls *Out of the Dust* by Karen Hesse

Oklahoma is one of only two states whose CAPITAL CITY'S NAME INCLUDES THE STATE NAME. (The other is Indianapolis, Indiana.)

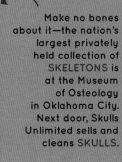

Make no bones about it—the nation's largest privately held collection of SKELETONS is at the Museum of Osteology in Oklahoma City. Next door, Skulls Unlimited sells and cleans SKULLS.

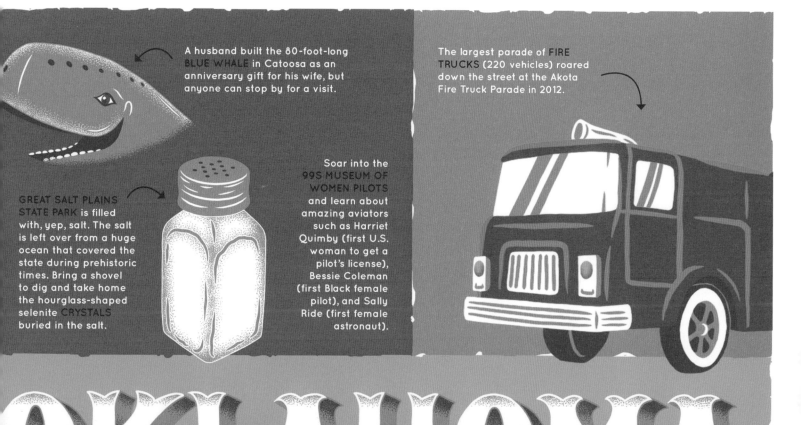

A husband built the 80-foot-long BLUE WHALE in Catoosa as an anniversary gift for his wife, but anyone can stop by for a visit.

The largest parade of FIRE TRUCKS (220 vehicles) roared down the street at the Akota Fire Truck Parade in 2012.

GREAT SALT PLAINS STATE PARK is filled with, yep, salt. The salt is left over from a huge ocean that covered the state during prehistoric times. Bring a shovel to dig and take home the hourglass-shaped selenite CRYSTALS buried in the salt.

Soar into the 99S MUSEUM OF WOMEN PILOTS and learn about amazing aviators such as Harriet Quimby (first U.S. woman to get a pilot's license), Bessie Coleman (first Black female pilot), and Sally Ride (first female astronaut).

OKLAHOMA

When the sky darkens and emergency sirens wail, Oklahomans take cover because a tornado is heading their way. A tornado (or "twister" as it's called here) is a powerful rotating column of air that can cause massive destruction and harm, and Oklahoma lives right in the "eye," or center, of Tornado Alley. The state holds the record for both the largest and the strongest tornadoes ever recorded. A tornado that touched down in El Reno in 2013 measured 2.6 miles wide (that's wider than Manhattan!). The NOAA National Severe Storms Laboratory, located in Oklahoma, works hard to keep everyone safe.

The Sooner State

Oklahoma's state capitol building is the only capitol with an OIL WELL under it.

SONIC DRIVE-IN began as a root beer stand in Shawnee in 1953. It's now a fast-food restaurant chain with carhops (waiters on roller skates) delivering food to cars. Every year at the SKATE-OFF, carhops carrying trays of food race through an obstacle course.

State Favorites   ICE CREAM FLAVOR Neapolitan • DESSERT fried pie • VEGETABLE okra

Bicyclists rule the roads in Oregon, a state populated with people who love fresh air, outdoor adventure, and care passionately about the environment. The city of Portland has the highest number of people who commute to work on two wheels. Fun pedaling events include the Flamingo Ride (people and bikes dress up as pink birds), Puppy-Palooza (dogs ride along), the Slowest Ride of the Year (led by unicycle), and the World Naked Bike Ride, which promotes bikes as a "green" way of transport!

Just north of Florence, take an elevator down to visit the hundreds of Stellar sea lions in the SEA LION CAVES, the nation's largest sea cave.

Oregon has the only TWO-SIDED STATE FLAG. The front shows a part of the state seal and there's a BEAVER on the back. Beavers were once plentiful in the state's rivers.

OREGON
The Beaver State

Mill Ends Park (two feet across) in Portland is the world's SMALLEST PARK and "the only LEPRECHAUN colony west of Ireland." Visitors have left a tiny swimming pool and Ferris wheel for the invisible leprechauns.

THOR'S WELL is also called the "Drainpipe of the Pacific." The bowl-shaped hole in the coastal rock appears to be constantly filling and "draining" the ocean water.

Meet the pack of rare, snow-white ARCTIC WOLVES roaming the White Wolf Sanctuary in Tidewater.

Clackamas County grows the most CHRISTMAS TREES in the nation (along with North Carolina's Blue Ridge Mountains).

Boring, Oregon—along with Dull, Scotland, and Bland, Australia—hosts TRINITY OF TEDIUM festivities. (Yawn...)

Over 99% of all the nation's HAZELNUTS (or filberts) are grown in the Willamette Valley.

State Favorites   FRUIT pears · BURGER veggie · DESSERT marionberry pie

The Kam Wah Chung Company Building in the city of John Day houses the most complete collection of Chinese herbal medicine and artifacts from the flourishing CHINESE FRONTIER COMMUNITY of the late 1800s to mid 1900s. Ever get car sick? Eating GINGER is said to prevent motion sickness.

In 2020, Bob Evans, an Oregon elementary school teacher, broke the world record for SWUGGLING—swimming while juggling five balls 101 times.

Dick Fosbury created the FOSBURY FLOP—the method of flipping in the air to go back-first over the bar in high jump—while at Medford High School.

The HUMONGOUS FUNGUS in the Malheur National Forest is believed to be the world's largest living organism. The giant honey mushroom, which lives mostly underground, weighs more than three blue whales and could be as much as 8,650 years old.

The OLDEST SURVIVING SHOES were discovered in Fort Rock Cave in 1938. The sagebrush bark sandals are about 9,500 years old. They're on display at the Museum of Natural and Cultural History in Eugene.

In 2015, 1,203 people played a game of RED LIGHT/GREEN LIGHT at Willamette University in Salem!

Sawdust flies at the Oregon Divisional CHAINSAW CARVING Championship in Reedsport, as carvers create masterpieces out of ordinary logs.

FAST

CAPITAL Salem

FUNNY PLACE NAMES Boring, Bridal Veil, Brothers, Drain, Noon, Rainbow, Remote, Riddle, Sisters, Sodaville, Sweet Home, Zigzag

STATE SLANG SUNBREAK means the sun's finally broken through the clouds, and if you hear THE MOUNTAIN'S OUT in Portland, it's clear enough to see Mount Hood in the distance.

The **STATE QUARTER** features CRATER LAKE, the deepest lake in the U.S. and the ninth deepest in the world.

FANTASTIC FOODS
The dark-purple MARIONBERRY, created at Oregon State University by crossing two types of blackberries, makes a delicious pie filling.

Enormous DUNGENESS CRABS, caught along the rugged coastline, are served warm and dipped in melted butter.

COOL INVENTIONS
University of Oregon track-and-field coach Bill Bowerman used a waffle iron to create a TRACK SHOE with a ridged rubber sole. Bowerman's company with partner Phil Knight became NIKE in 1971. Portland State University student Carolyn Davidson designed their "swoosh" logo for only $35! Bowerman's also credited with introducing JOGGING to the U.S.

After downhill ski champion Hjalmar Hvam of Portland fell and broke his leg because his bindings kept his feet attached to his skis, he invented the SAFETY-RELEASE SKI BINDING in 1937.

BOOKS *Ramona Quimby, Age 8* by Beverly Cleary   *Piecing Me Together* by Renée Watson

The Mütter Museum in Philadelphia is all about MEDICAL ODDITIES. There's a collection of 2,374 objects that people swallowed by mistake, including mini-binoculars and a school attendance pin.

The town of Kennett Square—the "Mushroom Capital of America"—grows over a third of the nation's farmed MUSHROOMS.

Crunch on this—Pennsylvania produces 80% of the nation's PRETZELS and has the most POTATO CHIP companies.

TOMATO FIGHT! Hurl pulpy, rotten tomatoes at your friends and neighbors at the annual Pittston Tomato Festival.

FAST FACTS

CAPITAL Harrisburg

FUNNY PLACE NAMES Bird-in-Hand, Foot of Ten, Forty Fort, Panic, Pillow, Rough and Ready, Snow Shoe, Squirrel Hill, Unicorn (plus Apollo, PA is a palindrome!)

STATE SLANG
• "YOUS" (in eastern PA) and "YINZ" (in western PA) both mean "you all."

• A BUGGY is a grocery store cart or what the Amish (a Christian group known for their simple lifestyle) ride in.

The **STATE QUARTER** features the gold COMMONWEALTH STATUE on the state capitol dome and the KEYSTONE symbol. A keystone is the center stone in an arch that holds everything in place. Pennsylvania earned its nickname because it was so important to early American history (we're talking Declaration of Independence, the First Continental Congress, and Benjamin Franklin, to name a few).

PENNSYLVANIA 1787
VIRTUE LIBERTY INDEPENDENCE

FANTASTIC FOODS
• Philadelphians are passionate about their CHEESESTEAKS, hot sliced beef topped with melted cheese and sautéed onions stuffed into a hoagie (submarine-style) roll.

• SHOO-FLY PIE is a molasses cake baked into a pie crust. Some say the name came from Pennsylvania Dutch bakers "shoo-ing" away flies from the sweet pies cooling on windowsills.

COOL INVENTIONS
• Pittsburgh hotel porter Alfred L. Cralle noticed the servers using two spoons to get ice cream into bowls because it would stick to the spoons. In 1897, Cralle invented the one-handed ICE CREAM SCOOP, originally called the Ice Cream Mold and Disher.

• Philadelphia stationer Hymen Lipman was the first to combine the graphite PENCIL WITH A RUBBER ERASER in 1858.

• In 1982, Carnegie Mellon University professor Scott E. Fahlman invented the smiley-face EMOTICON or :-). Emoticons are punctuation marks, letters, and numbers used to create picture icons to display an emotion (emotion + icon = emoticon).

BOOKS *Dead End in Norvelt* by Jack Gantos • *Wolf Hollow* by Lauren Wolk

Pittsburgh is called the CITY OF BRIDGES because it has the most bridges (446) of any city in the world, including Venice, Italy!

It's against state law to CATCH A FISH WITH YOUR MOUTH. Say what?

Visitors can go on a creepy scavenger hunt at the EASTERN STATE PENITENTIARY, the notorious prison once home to criminal Al Capone.

The abandoned town of Centralia has been sitting on top of a BURNING COAL MINE since 1962.

At the annual LITTLE LEAGUE BASEBALL WORLD SERIES in Williamsport, teams of 10-to-12-year-olds from around the globe compete for baseball glory.

Pennsylvania is a candy land! Good & Plenty was first produced in 1893 in Philadelphia, and in 1894, Milton S. Hershey began making chocolate in Lancaster County. His Hershey's Milk Chocolate Bar became the nation's first mass-produced chocolate. Around the same time in Pittsburgh, David L. Clark was cooking up Clark and Zagnut bars. Candy corn, Reese's Peanut Butter Cups, marshmallow Peeps, Mike and Ike candies, the Whitman's Sampler . . . so many treats got their sweet start in this state!

PENNSYLVANIA

The Keystone State

The five-story HAINES SHOE HOUSE on Shoe House Road in York was built in 1948 by a millionaire shoe salesman. It now sells ice cream—not sure what that's all a-boot!

Milton S. Hershey built the town of Hershey and HERSHEYPARK (now a huge amusement park) for the employees of his chocolate factory.

Every February 2nd, or GROUNDHOG DAY, the eyes of the nation turn to Punxsutawney Phil, the famous weather-predicting groundhog. German settlers started the tradition in the 1800s. (Phil has only been right 40% of the time.)

On NEW YEAR'S EVE, Pennsylvania towns drop some wacky stuff: bologna (Lebanon), a wrench (Mechanicsburg), a marshmallow Peep (Bethlehem), pickles (Dillsburg), and an ice cream cake (McVeytown).

Enjoy a slice while checking out Pizza Brain's MUSEUM OF PIZZA CULTURE in Philadelphia.

State Favorites   SNACK Cracker Jack • DRINK Birch Beer • BREAKFAST dippy eggs

RHODE ISLAND

THE OCEAN STATE

Rhode Island is fun-sized! The state (which, by the way, is not a road or an actual island) measures 1,214 square miles and is the smallest in the nation. Around 425 Rhode Islands could fit inside Alaska (and yet the state has more people than Alaska). Rhode Island also sports the shortest state motto: "Hope." Because you can drive across Little Rhody in about an hour, it's easy to experience its awesome boating, beach days, and seafood feasts at once!

Called the "Sistine Chapel of America," Woonsocket's St. Ann Art and Cultural Center is home to one of North America's largest collections of .

Visit in Portsmouth, where more than 80 huge shrubs are shaped like animals and imaginary creatures.

The world's largest (fake) bug lives on the roof of New England Pest Control in Providence. The 58-foot is named "Nibbles Woodaway."

The White Horse Tavern in Newport opened in 1673, making it the OLDEST OPERATING RESTAURANT in the nation.

Rhode Island was considered the " Capital of America" in the 1890s. Today, visitors to the grave of accused vampire Mercy Brown in Exeter often leave behind plastic vampire teeth.

Gilbert Stuart of Saunderstown painted the portrait of George Washington on the . The portrait's unfinished, because the president died mid-painting in 1799.

Be a LIGHTHOUSE KEEPER for a day! You and your family can stay overnight in the Rose Island Lighthouse in Newport.

I squid you not—the Rhode Island Festival in Narragansett celebrates the official state appetizer.

STate Favorites

COOKIE espiros • **BREAKFAST** bolo lêvedos or Portuguese muffins • **PIZZA** pizza strips

Little Rhody

Newport sure likes to be first. The country's first outdoor POLO match (1876), the first U.S. National TENNIS Championship (1881), the first U.S. Open GOLF Tournament (1895), and the first Newport JAZZ Festival (1954) all happened here.

In the 1800s, Lime Rock Lighthouse keeper IDA LEWIS was called the "bravest woman in America." She rescued as many as 36 people from drowning.

Cumberland is the only place on Earth that CUMBERLANDITE, the state rock, has been found. The magnetic rock is often mistaken for meteor debris.

The world's largest SOCK was made in Providence in 2011. The 32 feet by 22 feet by 8 feet cream and brown sock resembled a "sock monkey" puppet.

Squash the competition! The world's heaviest GREEN SQUASH weighed in at 2,118 pounds in Warren in 2017.

SPEED LiMiT 12 MPH?

Watch the road in Rhode Island! In 1904, Newport handed out the country's first jail sentence for SPEEDING. The offender was driving a whopping 15 miles per hour.

FAST FACTS

CAPITAL Providence

FUNNY PLACE NAMES Chopmist, Common Fence Point, Moosup Valley, The Hummocks

STATE SLANG
• A QUAHOG is a large hard-shelled clam abundant in the state's bays.

• A DYNAMITE is a sloppy joe-like, meat-filled sandwich that started in Woonsocket.

The STATE QUARTER features a SAILBOAT gliding through Narragansett Bay by the Pell Bridge. The Ocean State is known as the nation's sailing capital.

FANTASTIC FOODS
• STUFFIES are made from chopped quahogs mixed with breadcrumbs, onions, and bell pepper, and stuffed into an empty clamshell then baked. Sometimes Portuguese sausage called CHOURIÇO is added.

• COFFEE MILK (the state drink) is milk mixed with coffee-flavored syrup. A COFFEE CABINET isn't a piece of furniture, but a coffee-syrup, milk, and ice cream milkshake. It may have got its name because a blender (used to make the shake) is kept in a kitchen cabinet.

• HOT WIENERS (or New York System Wieners) are not hot dogs. They're made, instead, with veal and pork and served "all the way" in a steamed bun with meat sauce, yellow mustard, chopped onion, and celery salt.

COOL INVENTIONS
• The toy MR. POTATO HEAD was invented by George Lerner in 1949 and manufactured by Hasbro in Pawtucket. Kids originally stuck the plastic body parts into a REAL potato! The famous spud was the first toy to be advertised on television.

• Governor and Civil War general Ambrose Burnside had thick cheek whiskers that people used to call "burnsides." Later, the name was reversed to SIDEBURNS.

BOOKS Something Upstairs by Avi • The Art of the Swap by Kristine Asselin and Jen Malone

Cooking up Frogmore stew is the perfect reason to gather family and friends for a laid-back, sip-sweet-tea-on-the-front-porch South Carolina day. Frogmore stew is one of the most famous meals in the Lowcountry, the southern coast, and sea islands of South Carolina. But get this—there are no frogs in Frogmore stew, and it's not a stew. A one-pot meal of spicy shrimp (always plentiful in the tidal creeks), corn on the cob, new potatoes, and smoked sausage, it's best enjoyed outside on a newspaper-covered table in the welcome shade of live oaks dripping with Spanish moss.

Myrtle Beach is known as the MINI-GOLF Capital of the World with over 50 courses.

At the ROLLING IN THE GRITS contest in St. George, contestants dive into a grits-filled pool and whoever comes out wearing the most grits after 10 seconds wins.

Morgan Island is only for MONKEYS. Over 4,000 rhesus macaques live on the island, and the only humans allowed are primate researchers. A true Planet of the Apes!

The Palmetto State

SOUTH CAROLINA

The Carolina Reaper is the HOTTEST PEPPER in the world.

STUMPHOUSE TUNNEL, an abandoned railroad shortcut near Isaqueena Falls, was taken over for a few years in the 1950s by Clemson University to grow stinky BLUE CHEESE!

When Dalton King couldn't sleep, he started sewing BUTTONS onto his clothes. Soon he was covering everything in buttons, opening the Button King Museum in Bishopville.

The 135-foot PEACHOID water tower in Gaffney has been the "butt" of many jokes.

At 40 feet tall, Eddie is the BIGGEST KID IN THE WORLD! You can crawl inside his brain and slide down his intestines at Columbia's EdVenture Children's Museum.

A man in Bowman built a UFO WELCOME CENTER to give aliens a comfy place to hang out if they ever decide to land in South Carolina.

State Favorites

SNACK boiled peanuts • DESSERT coconut cake • COOKIE benne wafer

Coiled SWEETGRASS BASKETS, woven by the Gullah Geechee people of the Lowcountry, are one of the oldest surviving African art forms in the U.S.

Seeing the primitive dental tools at the Macaulay Museum of DENTAL HISTORY in Charleston will help visitors remember to floss daily!

Pig out at the CHITLIN' STRUT festival in Salley. Chitlins (or chitterlings) are fried hog intestines.

In May 1865, thousands of formerly enslaved Charleston residents held a parade to honor Union soldiers who'd died in the Civil War. Many historians mark this as one of the earliest MEMORIAL DAY ceremonies.

The largest collection of TOASTERS (1,284 as of 2012) belongs to Kenneth Huggins of Columbia.

A statue of children's book character AMELIA BEDELIA stands in Manning, hometown of author Peggy Parish.

FAST FACTS

CAPITAL Columbia

FUNNY PLACE NAMES Due West, Fair Play, Green Sea, Ketchuptown, Mars Bluff, Mayo, Ninety Six, Pumpkintown, Round O, Spiderweb

STATE SLANG
If you hear, "I RECKON I MIGHT COULD do that," when you ask someone to do something, they mean "maybe" or there's a possibility they'll do it.

The **STATE QUARTER** features the PALMETTO (state tree), YELLOW JESSAMINE (state flower), and CAROLINA WREN (state bird). A male Carolina wren's loud song sounds like "teakettle-teakettle."

FANTASTIC FOODS
SHRIMP AND GRITS was originally a fisherman's hearty breakfast and is now served at fancy restaurants. Grits are stone-ground corn boiled until soft and then combined with butter, milk, and sometimes cheese.

HOPPIN' JOHN (it's unclear where the name came from!) is black-eyed peas (or field peas) cooked slowly with bacon or ham and served over rice. South Carolinians believe eating Hoppin' John and collard greens on New Year's Day brings good luck. The peas represent coins, and some families hide a real penny or dime in the peas before serving them.

COOL INVENTIONS
The very first SUBMARINE to sink an enemy ship was the *H.L. Hunley* (named after inventor Horace Hunley) in the Charleston Harbor during the Civil War. Encased in a metal tube with no engine and no oxygen supply, the crew had to watch the candle they used for light. When the flame went out, it meant they were out of oxygen and needed to rise to the surface FAST for air.

BOOKS *Brown Girl Dreaming* by Jacqueline Woodson *The Parker Inheritance* by Varian Johnson

SOUTH DAKOTA

Want to go digging for dinosaurs? South Dakota is a great place to start. Millions of years ago, dinosaurs and other prehistoric animals roamed its Black Hills, Badlands, and vast prairies. One of the largest and most complete skeletons of a Tyrannosaurus rex was discovered near Faith. It was named "Sue," after Sue Hendrickson, the amateur fossil-hunter who found it. In 2020, a 3,000-pound triceratops skull was unearthed by a group of college students. They named it "Shady," after the nearby town of Shadehill. If you found a dinosaur, what would you name it?

PIERRE, SOUTH DAKOTA, is the only combination of U.S. state and capital that doesn't share any letters.

A-maizing! The world's only CORN PALACE, built in Mitchell in 1892, is covered by 3,500 bushels of corn that are replaced every spring.

Reptile Gardens near Rapid City is the world's largest REPTILE ZOO.

The mascot of the INTERNATIONAL VINEGAR MUSEUM is . . . a pickle!

Clark is home to a famous MASHED POTATO WRESTLING contest.

Aberdeen locals hand out free PHEASANT SALAD SANDWICHES to hunters arriving in town, a tradition started when U.S. troops passed through Aberdeen on trains during World War II.

The granite mountain carving of Lakota leader CRAZY HORSE upon his steed is in progress in the Black Hills and should be one of the world's largest sculptures (563 feet high, 641 feet long) when finished.

The LARGEST HAILSTONE recovered in the U.S. fell near the town of Vivian in 2010—it was nearly the size of a volleyball!

Electrifying! It's against the law in Huron to cause STATIC between 7:00 a.m. and 11:00 p.m.

South Dakota and North Dakota grow most of the nation's SUNFLOWERS. Did you know the head of the sunflower is a combination of a thousand tiny flowers?

State Favorites

PIZZA TOPPING bacon · COOKIE spritz cookie · DESSERT kuchen

THE MOUNT RUSHMORE STATE

South Dakota's ORIGINAL 1880 TOWN in Midland is the town that time forgot—it looks exactly like it did back then!

The faces of presidents George Washington, Thomas Jefferson, Theodore Roosevelt, and Abraham Lincoln were sculpted into MOUNT RUSHMORE in 1941. Around 90% of the carving was done by dynamite.

The Conata Basin and Badlands National Park are working to restore the population of BLACK-FOOTED FERRETS, one of the most endangered land mammals and the only ferret native to the U.S.

It's a flush to the finish line at the TOILET BOWL RACES (two toilets on wheels steered by plungers), part of Centerville's whirlwind Tornado Days celebration.

Sturgis is a motorcycle mecca, hosting the STURGIS MOTORCYCLE RALLY since the 1930s. Some bikers compete for the hairy crown in the BEARD AND MUSTACHE CONTEST.

Since the 1930s, WALL DRUG STORE has been a popular stop on long, hot prairie road trips because they offer free ice water to travelers. Out front stands an enormous statue of a JACKALOPE (a jackrabbit with antelope horns), South Dakota's most famous mythical creature.

FAST FACTS

CAPITAL Pierre

FUNNY PLACE NAMES
Camp Crook, Deadwood, Plenty Bears, Running Water, Tea, Thunder Butte, Wall, Winner

STATE SLANG
• DINNER is the noon meal or lunch, and SUPPER is the evening meal.

• "I PERT'NEAR finished my homework," means "almost" or "pretty near."

The STATE QUARTER features the CHINESE RING-NECKED PHEASANT in flight above the MOUNT RUSHMORE National Memorial. Thousands of pheasants make their home in South Dakota's endless prairies and wheat fields. Did you know a group of pheasants is called a bouquet?

SOUTH DAKOTA 1889

FANTASTIC FOODS
• CHISLIC, the official "state nosh," is cubes of fried, salted meat served on wooden skewers with crackers on the side. The dish was first introduced by Russian immigrants.

• FRY BREAD, the official state bread, was created by Native nations. Pillows of dough are fried until crispy on the outside and soft on the inside. INDIAN TACOS are tacos on fry bread.

COOL INVENTIONS
• South Dakota State University's Dairy Bar is said to have invented COOKIES 'N' CREAM ice cream in 1979.

BOOKS A Boy Called Slow by Joseph Bruchac • Prairie Lotus by Linda Sue Park

The PARTHENON in Nashville (built in 1897 as an art gallery) is the world's only full-scale replica of the Parthenon in Athens, Greece.

Go bananas for the ultimate Southern treat at the national BANANA PUDDING festival in Centerville.

DOLLYWOOD, singer Dolly Parton's theme park in Pigeon Forge, serves a 25-pound APPLE PIE baked in a cast-iron skillet. One slice is big enough to feed a whole family!

Tennessee (along with Missouri) BORDERS THE MOST OTHER STATES: Kentucky, Virginia, North Carolina, Arkansas, Missouri, Georgia, Mississippi, and Alabama.

The NATIONAL CIVIL RIGHTS MUSEUM in Memphis doesn't look like a museum, because it's housed in the motel where Dr. Martin Luther King, Jr. was assassinated on April 4th, 1968.

FAST FACTS

CAPITAL Nashville

FUNNY PLACE NAMES Bucksnort, Bugscuffle, Difficult, Dismal, Flippin, Hanging Limb, Nameless, Only, Soddy-Daisy, Suck-egg Hollow, Sweet Lips, Yum Yum

STATE SLANG

• If the milk is **BLINKED**, it's spoiled.

• A **CATHEAD** is a flaky buttermilk biscuit (as big as a cat's head!).

• If someone's feeling **PUNY**, they're feeling sick or not their usual self.

The **STATE QUARTER** features three musical instruments—**GUITAR**, **TRUMPET**, and **FIDDLE**—to represent the three popular types of music: country (Nashville), blues (Memphis), and bluegrass (the Eastern mountains).

FANTASTIC FOODS

• **HOT CHICKEN** is sure to set your mouth on fire! This fried chicken is super-spiced with cayenne pepper. For a true Nashville experience, eat it on a slice of white bread with pickle chips.

• **COUNTRY HAM** with **RED-EYE GRAVY** and **CORNBREAD** is a Southern specialty. The gravy is made with ham drippings and coffee.

COOL INVENTIONS

• The first **COTTON CANDY MACHINE** was invented in 1897 by a Nashville dentist (yep, a DENTIST!), Dr. William Morrison, and candy maker John C. Wharton. They called their sugar-spun treat "Fairy Floss."

• After six men spent eight hours pulling a friend's car from a river, Chattanooga's Ernest Holmes Sr. decided there had to be a better way and invented the **TOW TRUCK** in 1916. The International Towing and Recovery Hall of Fame & Museum is in Chattanooga.

BOOKS A Snicker of Magic by Natalie Lloyd • Paperboy by Vince Vawter

The SALT AND PEPPER SHAKER Museum spices up life in Gatlinburg with over 20,000 sets in all shapes and sizes.

The first CRACKER BARREL restaurant, opened by Dan Evins in 1969 in Lebanon, was decorated to look like an old Tennessee country store. In the late 1800s, country stores all had big barrels filled with crackers that customers would gather around to chat.

Every year at ELVIS WEEK at Graceland (the mansion of singer Elvis Presley) hundreds of tribute artists compete to be crowned "Ultimate Elvis."

Camden is home to North America's only FRESHWATER PEARL farm. The iridescent official state gem is formed inside the washboard mussel.

GREAT SMOKY MOUNTAINS NATIONAL PARK is the nation's most visited national park.

TENNESSEE

Music isn't part of the culture in Tennessee—it *is* the culture. In Memphis, Delta blues and soul grew popular on Beale Street, and Elvis Presley ignited the flame of rock 'n' roll at Sun Studio. Meanwhile, country music performed on Nashville stages traveled via radio into living rooms across the country. The Grand Ole Opry has had the nation's longest-running live radio broadcast since 1925. And every year, aspiring musicians and songwriters travel to Tennessee (just as Taylor Swift did when she was 14) to pursue their starry dreams.

THE VOLUNTEER STATE

Piggly Wiggly, founded in Memphis in 1916, was the country's FIRST SELF-SERVICE GROCERY STORE. Before this, shoppers gave written orders to a clerk who'd collect the goods from the store shelves. The Pink Palace Museum features a replica of the first store.

LITTLE DEBBIE is real. She was the granddaughter of the founders of the Tennessee snack cake company, Little Debbie.

You'll never meet a SEEING EYE DOG today named Buddy. Seeing Eye founder Morris Frank trained the first guide dog for the blind—a German Shepherd named Buddy—in Nashville in 1928. Frank eventually had six dogs all named Buddy and, in their honor, The Seeing Eye retired the name.

State Favorites

FRUIT tomato • CANDY Goo Goo Clusters • BREAKFAST sweet potato pancakes

Texas is famous for oil wells, cowboys, cattle, and Tex-Mex food. Tex-Mex, not to be confused with authentic Mexican food (salsa, tomatillos, tamales, and enchiladas), is a fusion of Spanish, Native, Mexican, and American cuisines and often contains plenty of cheese. Fajitas, nachos, and chili con queso are pure Tex-Mex goodness. Chili con carne made with hearty chunks of beef (never beans!) is the Lone Star State's official food, and "chiliheads" (intense fans) vie at cook-offs throughout the state.

The TALLEST BLUEBONNET FLOWER (64.75 inches tall) was discovered in Big Bend National Park in 2005.

Paris, Texas, has its own EIFFEL TOWER— but with a cowboy hat on top!

Nearly the size of a tennis court and containing almost a ton of butter, the world's largest GINGERBREAD HOUSE was constructed in Bryan in 2013.

TEXAS
THE LONE STAR STATE

Hidalgo, called the KILLER BEE Capital of the World, has a buzz-worthy 2,000-pound bee sculpture. In the 1950s, Brazilian scientists were engineering a bee that would produce more honey, and some of these aggressive bees escaped and swarmed north. Hidalgo was their first U.S. stop.

You can literally lick the walls of Grand Saline's SALT PALACE MUSEUM because they're built out of salt blocks. Grand Saline sits on top of one of the nation's largest and purest salt domes.

KING RANCH, located in Kingsville, is larger than the state of Rhode Island.

In Cedar Creek, there's a vending machine always stocked with full-sized homemade PECAN PIES.

Try your luck (or cluck!) at the East Texas Poultry Festival's CHICKEN CLUCKING CONTEST.

BARNEY SMITH'S TOILET SEAT ART MUSEUM at The Colony near Dallas displays 1,400 seats decorated by a former plumber.

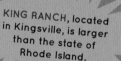

State Favorites

SANDWICH chopped brisket · SNACK salsa & chips · BREAKFAST migas

CADILLAC RANCH in Amarillo is an art installation of 10 graffiti-covered Cadillacs buried nose-first in a field. You're allowed to bring paint to add to the graffiti!

"Howdy, folks!" BIG TEX has boomed to visitors at the State Fair of Texas in Dallas since 1952. The world's tallest cowboy stands an incredible 55 feet high, wears a 95-gallon hat and size 96 boots!

Have a spare minute? Strike out for the International BOWLING Museum and Hall of Fame in Arlington.

No one will die from boredom at the National Museum of FUNERAL HISTORY in Houston. There's memorabilia from famous funerals, a hearse collection, and displays of Dia de Los Muertos traditions.

The NINE-BANDED ARMADILLO, the official state small mammal, always gives birth to four identical quadruplets.

In 1929, the accidental discovery of a red grapefruit growing on a pink grapefruit tree in the Rio Grande Valley led to the creation of the sweet RUBY RED GRAPEFRUIT.

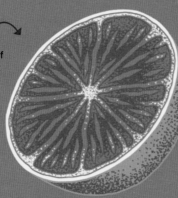

The holiday JUNETEENTH, celebrating Black emancipation, had its start in Texas. Juneteenth is short for June Nineteenth, and at many festivals and family cook-outs strawberry soda and red velvet cake are served.

FAST FACTS

CAPITAL Austin

FUNNY PLACE NAMES Belcherville, Bigfoot, Chocolate Bayou, Circle Back, Cuthand, Ding Dong, Earth, Goodnight, Jot Em Down, My Large Intestine, Muleshoe, Needmore, Noodle, Oatmeal, Pancake, Río Frío, Sour Lake

STATE SLANG

• If someone is ALL HAT, NO CATTLE, it means they brag a lot but don't have much to show for it.

• Something that's "as good AS ALL GIT-OUT" is the best ever.

The STATE QUARTER features a ROPE (to represent the state's cowboy history) and a FIVE-POINTED STAR. In 1836, Texas won independence from Mexico to become its own republic, and was made a U.S. state in 1845. Students in the state recite two pledges every morning —the American and the Texan.

FANTASTIC FOODS

• Many states claim to have the best barbecue, but none have juicy BRISKET—a smoky, tender slab of beef—like Texas.

• Everything's big in Texas including COWBOY COOKIES, packed with oats, pecans, chocolate chips, and coconut flakes.

• KOLACHES are pastries filled with apricot, prune, poppy seed, or sweet cheese and were introduced by Czech immigrants.

COOL INVENTIONS

• The soft drink DR PEPPER was originally called a "Waco" because this is where it was invented by pharmacist Charles Alderton in 1885. The city is now home to a Dr Pepper Museum.

• In 1967, Herb Kelleher and Rollin King developed SOUTHWEST AIRLINES while having dinner, and wrote their business plan on a napkin. They drew a triangle to show how they'd fly between Dallas, Houston, and San Antonio.

BOOKS *Holes* by Louis Sachar • *The Evolution of Calpurnia Tate* by Jacqueline Kelly

The landscape of Utah is decorated by the most amazing otherworldly natural formations. Defying gravity, hoodoos (also called goblins and fairy chimneys) are tall spires of rock with mushroom-shaped caps. Deep slot canyons seem to conceal hidden worlds in their narrow gulches. And the blazing-white, lunar-like Bonneville Salt Flats were formed thousands of years ago when a huge body of water evaporated. Arches, sandstone cliffs, salt lakes, buttes . . . Utah's unique beauty goes on and on.

UTAH
The Beehive State

Grab goggles and a swimsuit for Thanksgiving Point's Jigglefest JELL-O FOOD FIGHT! Utahns consume the most JELL-O per capita in the nation.

A 25-foot wooden WATERMELON SLICE marks the celebration of Melon Days in Green River, Utah's prime melon-growing spot.

You'll naturally float in the GREAT SALT LAKE because the very salty water makes your body buoyant.

With a 290-foot span, LANDSCAPE ARCH in Arches National Park is the nation's longest natural rock arch.

Home sweet cave! The 14-room HOLE 'N' THE ROCK HOUSE in Moab was carved directly into the sandstone.

The state holiday PIONEER DAY on July 24th commemorates the arrival of Mormon pioneers, led by Brigham Young, into the Salt Lake Valley in 1847.

Have you ever loved a movie so much you wanted to magically go into the screen and live there? One Herriman family had that dream and built the UP HOUSE from the Disney-Pixar movie!

Park City is the BIGGEST SKI RESORT in the U.S., with 39 ski lifts. On its license plates, Utah claims to have "THE GREATEST SNOW ON EARTH."

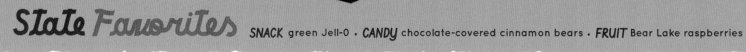

State Favorites

SNACK green Jell-O · CANDY chocolate-covered cinnamon bears · FRUIT Bear Lake raspberries

Spring brings a rainbow of colored powder to Sri Sri Radha Krishna Temple in Spanish Fork, the hosts of the nation's largest HOLI FESTIVAL.

Dig for and take home any 500-million-year-old TRILOBITE FOSSIL you find at the U-Dig fossil site in the Great Basin Desert, one of the richest deposits of trilobites on Earth.

At the MARS DESERT RESEARCH STATION, researchers pretend they're isolated on the Red Planet and study what humans will need to do to survive on Mars. They even wear spacesuits to go outside!

During SPEED WEEK on the Bonneville Salt Flats, land speed records are broken by trucks, motorcycles, and streamliners racing faster than 500 miles per hour.

The staff at Salt Lake City's United States Postal Service Remote Encoding Center READ THE UNREADABLE! Every piece of U.S. mail with a messy, scribbled address that postal machines can't read is deciphered by a human.

PANDO is a group of quaking aspen trees in Richfield that share a single root system. It's one of the world's oldest and heaviest living organisms, spreading over 100 acres of land. "Pando" is Latin for "I spread."

Lee Redmond from Salt Lake City set the record for the LONGEST FINGERNAILS in 2008 at 28 feet, 4 inches! A year later, she broke her nails in a car accident.

FAST FACTS

CAPITAL Salt Lake City

FUNNY PLACE NAMES
American Fork, Birdseye, Bonanza, Centerfield, Echo, Helper, Hideout, Hurricane, Mexican Hat, Plain City

STATE SLANG
• "I'm **SLUFFING** for a **POWDER DAY**," means you're skipping school to go skiing.

The **STATE QUARTER** features two trains facing the **GOLDEN SPIKE** that joined the tracks of the Central Pacific and Union Pacific railroads in 1869 at Promontory, Utah. Before cars and airplanes, the First Transcontinental Railroad was the quickest way to travel across the country.

FANTASTIC FOODS
• **UTAH SCONES** are like fry bread or sopaipillas, except the fried dough is slathered with whipped honey butter.

• **PASTRAMI BURGERS** are beef patties topped with pastrami, lettuce, fry sauce (made with ketchup and mayonnaise), onions, tomato, and cheese.

• It's no surprise that **FUNERAL POTATOES**—a baked casserole made with potatoes, canned soup, cheese, and a crushed corn-flake or potato chip topping—got its name because it was served at funerals.

COOL INVENTIONS
• Nolan Bushnell, known as the "Father of Electronic Gaming," developed **PONG** in 1972, kickstarting a national love of **VIDEO GAMES**. He also created Atari, the company that brought video games into homes, and the restaurant chain Chuck E. Cheese.

BOOKS *Real Friends* by Shannon Hale • *Palace Beautiful* by Sarah DeFord Williams

In Vermont, there's one COW for every 2.4 Vermonters!

Say cheese! Cabot Creamery cooked the world's largest GRILLED CHEESE SANDWICH (320 pounds) in 2000 and the world's largest MAC & CHEESE (2,469 pounds) in 2010.

PEE-EWWW! The ODOR-EATERS ROTTEN SNEAKER CONTEST started in Montpelier, but now kids nationwide submit their stinky sneakers to win big prizes!

Most of the granite headstones used in U.S. cemeteries come from the ROCK OF AGES GRANITE QUARRY in Graniteville.

FAST FACTS

CAPITAL Montpelier

FUNNY PLACE NAMES Adamant, Bread Loaf, Butternut Bend Falls, Goose Green, Hardscrabble Corner, Lazy Lady Island, Mosquitoville, Skunks Misery Road, Tinmouth

STATE SLANG

• If something is **DOWN CELLAR**, it's in the basement.

• **CHININ'** is short for "snow machining," which is snowmobiling.

• **CREEMEE** is soft serve ice cream.

The **STATE QUARTER** features **MAPLE TREES** being tapped for syrup in front of Camel's Hump mountain. A little device (like a water spigot) is used to collect the sap, which is brought to a building called the sugar house and boiled down until it becomes thick syrup. It takes about 40 cups of sap to make one cup of maple syrup.

FANTASTIC FOODS

• **SUGAR ON SNOW** is maple syrup heated up then ladled over clean, packed snow where it hardens like taffy. Then it's eaten together with sour pickles and plain doughnuts!

• **APPLE PIE WITH CHEDDAR CHEESE** is a dessert that's often eaten for breakfast. There's a Vermont saying: "Apple pie without the cheese is like a hug without the squeeze."

COOL INVENTIONS

• America's first **GLOBE FACTORY** was created in 1813 by James Wilson, a self-taught farmer from Bradford. After seeing globes at Dartmouth College, he decided to make his own and read books to teach himself geography and mapmaking.

BOOKS *The Brilliant Fall of Gianna Z.* by Kate Messner • *Small Spaces* by Katherine Arden

To view the stars at the Hartness-Porter MUSEUM OF AMATEUR TELESCOPE MAKING, visitors go through an underground tunnel in a historic mansion in Springfield.

There have been hundreds of sightings of CHAMP, the mythic LAKE MONSTER living in Lake Champlain.

For 18 days in 1998, LAKE CHAMPLAIN became the sixth Great Lake, after a Vermont Member of Congress slipped the title into a bill. Upon discovery, the lake was bumped back to a regular lake.

Ice cream company Ben & Jerry's sends its retired flavors to the FLAVOR GRAVEYARD. The "dearly de-pinted" each get a headstone and epitaph in a real graveyard at the company's factory in Waterbury.

PEANUTS, POPCORN!
MIX 'EM IN A POT!
PLOP 'EM IN YOUR ICE CREAM?
WELL, MAYBE NOT.

Vermonters are great recyclers! A retired schoolteacher created VERMONTASAURUS, a 122-foot-long and 25-foot-high dinosaur sculpture made entirely of scrap wood.

Smugglers' Notch boasts the East's only TRIPLE-BLACK DIAMOND ski trail, the Black Hole. A single black diamond indicates an expert slope. Now multiply that by three!

On GREEN UP DAY, on the first Saturday of May, Vermonters of all ages clean miles of roadside trash.

The VERMONT TEDDY BEAR factory in Shelburne has a teddy bear hospital to repair "injured" bears.

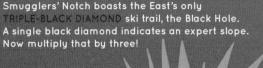

VERMONT

THE GREEN MOUNTAIN STATE

Maple is the flavor of Vermont. The "Green Mountain State" is the nation's largest producer of pure maple syrup, and Vermonters pour it on absolutely everything— pancakes, ice cream, coffee, popcorn, cotton candy, meat, and vegetables too. Maple syrup lovers can visit St. Albans for a sweet time at the Vermont Maple Festival and stop at the New England Maple Museum in Pittsford (you can't miss it—there's a 1,700-gallon jug of syrup out front) to learn the 200-year history of maple sugaring.

To cross Sunset Lake, cars drive on the Brookfield FLOATING BRIDGE, which sits on top of the water.

Both the largest and the strangest-looking GILFEATHER TURNIPS take home prizes at the Gilfeather Turnip Festival in Wardsboro.

The Von Trapp family, made famous in the movie THE SOUND OF MUSIC, moved to Stowe because it reminded them of their Alpine home in Austria.

DEAD BUG ART decorates the walls of the Fairbanks Museum in St. Johnsbury. Artist John Hampson used thousands of beetles, moths, and butterflies to create beautiful mosaics.

State Favorites ICE CREAM FLAVOR maple walnut • FRUIT apple • BREAKFAST granola

If you've ever eaten peanuts at a baseball game, they were probably grown in Virginia. Virginia peanuts are extra-flavorful, extra-large, and extra-crunchy. Did you know peanuts aren't really nuts? They're legumes, like peas. Peanuts (also called "goobers") were brought to North America from Central and South America and Africa, and planted in Virginia. The First Peanut Museum in Waverly serves up gobs of goober history. For example, a farmer in Virginia named Benjamin Hicks is credited for cracking the shell off the peanut industry in the 1890s by inventing a machine that made harvesting and cleaning peanuts so much easier. Pass the peanuts!

FOAMHENGE in Centreville is a Styrofoam replica of Stonehenge, the circle of ancient stones in England.

At the Woodbooger Festival in Norton, grab a flashlight for a nighttime hunt through the southwestern Virginia woods in search of WOODBOOGER, a Bigfoot-like creature.

VIRGINIA

The Old Dominion

At the Richmond International DRAGON BOAT FESTIVAL, teams of paddlers race along the James River in long canoes decorated to look like dragons. A drummer sitting in front gives the paddlers a steady beat.

The LONGEST GUM WRAPPER CHAIN (over 20 miles!) was constructed by Gary Duschl in Virginia Beach in 2020. He worked on it for two hours a day, every day, since 1965.

In the mid-1800s, before trains had dining cars, women sold FRIED CHICKEN to train passengers passing through Gordonsville. Back then, the town was called the "Chicken-Leg Center of the Universe." Today, it hosts a famous Fried Chicken Festival.

The MAGGIE L. WALKER NATIONAL HISTORIC SITE in Richmond celebrates an inspirational civil rights and community leader, newspaper editor, and bank president. Walker was the nation's first Black woman to run a bank, the St. Luke Penny Savings Bank, in 1903.

STATE Favorites   ICE CREAM tiger tail · BREAKFAST biscuit with apple butter · DESSERT hot milk cake

Luray Caverns is home to the world's largest musical instrument, the GREAT STALACPIPE ORGAN. Created by engineer Leland W. Sprinkle (best name ever!), the stalactites (a geological formation created by dripping water) are tapped with mallets connected to an organ keyboard. It's believed Sprinkle got the idea after his son hit his head on a stalactite, and they heard the cave hum!

Naval Station Norfolk is the world's largest NAVAL STATION, supporting 75 ships and 134 aircraft, alongside 14 piers and 11 aircraft hangars.

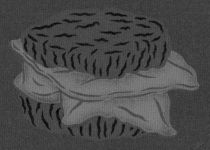

Ham it up in Smithfield! The town created the world's (2,200 pounds) in 2002, and keeps the world's (dating back to 1902) at their Isle of Wight County Museum. You can spy on the ham from your home with their 24/7 !

The locals of remote TANGIER ISLAND in the Chesapeake Bay, originally settled by British colonists in the 1680s, still speak with what sounds like a British accent.

Every July, "Saltwater Cowboys" on horseback round up about 150 wild ponies from Assateague Island and swim them to Chincoteague Island. The first foal to reach shore is named King or Queen Neptune.

FAST FACTS

CAPITAL Richmond

FUNNY PLACE NAMES Bland, Bleak, Bumpass, Cuckoo, Fries, Goose Pimple Junction, Gore, Meadows of Dan, Nicelytown, Spotsylvania Courthouse, Stinking Point, Tightsqueeze, Tiptop

STATE SLANG

• STAMP is the same as promising or swearing you did something, such as, "I stamp I studied for the test."

• DMV stands for D.C., Maryland, and Virginia. NOVA is Northern Virginia.

The STATE QUARTER features the three ships that brought English colonists to JAMESTOWN in the spring of 1607, to form the first permanent English settlement in what would eventually become the U.S.

FANTASTIC FOODS

• Creamy PEANUT SOUP, made with peanuts or peanut butter and onions, celery, chicken stock, and cream, has its roots in West African cuisine.

• BRUNSWICK STEW was first made in the early 1800s, and the savory tomato-based vegetable stew used to contain squirrel, opossum, or rabbit meat. Today they've been replaced with chicken, pork, or beef, but the stew is still often cooked in a huge cast-iron cauldron and stirred with a boat oar.

COOL INVENTIONS

• In the late 1890s, Dr. Charles Browne Fleet of Lynchburg invented CHAPSTICK, but it looked like a candle wrapped in tinfoil, so no one bought it. He sold his invention for five dollars to his friend John Morton, and Morton's wife repackaged the pink lip balm in brass tubes. From then on, the business was a smooth success.

BOOKS *Bridge to Terabithia* by Katherine Paterson • *Misty of Chincoteague* by Marguerite Henry

WASHINGTON

THE EVERGREEN STATE

Watch out for flying fish! Fishmongers at Seattle's Pike Place Market fling wild salmon and other local fish from the ice-packed display cases in the front onto the scales in the back. Born in the state's freshwater streams, salmon migrate to the Pacific Ocean then swim upstream to return home. The super-popular (yet increasingly endangered) pink fish is enjoyed cooked on cedar planks, smoked into jerky, mashed into burgers, or raw in sushi. And there's also salmon candy—smoked salmon cured with brown sugar and drenched in maple syrup. We're hooked!

It's illegal to throw food in the trash in Seattle. Be sure to toss it in a COMPOST BIN.

There's a GARBAGE-EATING GOAT in Spokane! The steel goat sculpture "eats" paper trash and a vacuum inside "swallows" it.

Since the 1990s, passers-by have added wads of chewed gum and coins to Seattle's huge GUM WALL. Gum walls are one of the nation's germiest attractions (no surprise there!).

Try SWEET ONION BOWLING at the Walla Walla Sweet Onion Festival. Walla Walla is a First Nations' name meaning "many waters," and its wet valley is the perfect place to grow the state veggie.

The very first STARBUCKS coffee shop opened in Seattle's Pike Place Market in 1971.

Washington operates the largest FERRY system in the U.S. Most routes cross the Puget Sound.

The Leavenworth NUTCRACKER Museum displays thousands of the toy soldiers made famous by the holiday ballet.

The Pacific Bonsai Museum in Federal Way blooms with living, leafy sculptures. An ancient Japanese art form with Chinese roots, BONSAI is a small tree that's grown in a container to look like a large tree.

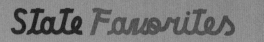

State Favorites

COOKIE apple cinnamon · FRUIT Rainier cherries · CANDY Fran's chocolates

Nicknamed the LAVENDER Capital of North America, Sequim is carpeted in fragrant purple flowers every summer. Try some lavender ice cream and lavender fudge.

A feline field trip to MEOWTROPOLITAN CAT CAFE in Seattle allows you to snuggle with adoptable cats at this purr-fect coffee shop.

Found in the Puget Sound, GEODUCKS (pronounced "gooey-ducks") are the largest burrowing clams in the world with a neck, or siphon, that's up to three feet long.

Minty fresh! Washington is the top MINT-producing state. Just one drop of mint oil can flavor a full tube of toothpaste.

It takes 43 seconds by elevator to reach the observation deck of the famous Seattle SPACE NEEDLE, or you can climb 848 stairs to the top. Your choice.

Are you a Lord of the Rings fan? Many HOBBIT HOUSES are tucked into the state's woods.

Why did the chicken cross the road? To get to Seattle's RUBBER CHICKEN MUSEUM, home of the world's largest and smallest rubber chickens.

Washington is the nation's top grower of APPLES. If all the apples picked in one year in the state were placed side-by-side, they'd circle the Earth 29 times.

FAST FACTS

CAPITAL Olympia

FUNNY PLACE NAMES Big Bottom, Country Homes, Dollar Corner, Dynamite, George (get it?), Kid Valley, Medical Lake, Mold, Soap Lake

STATE SLANG

• **LIQUID SUNSHINE** describes a day that starts out sunny, but ends up rainy. Locals never carry an umbrella. They wear parkas or just get wet.

• A **SEATTLE TUXEDO** is a flannel shirt or a fleece paired with jeans.

• A **FLOAT HOUSE** is a houseboat. Some Seattle luxury houseboats can cost millions!

The **STATE QUARTER** features a leaping **SALMON** with **MOUNT RAINIER** in the background. Covered by glaciers and snowfields, Mount Rainier is considered an active volcano, although it hasn't erupted since 1894.

FANTASTIC FOODS

• **RHUBARB PIE** is a sweet pie made with a tart vegetable. Washington is one of the nation's largest producers of rhubarb.

• Washington boasts amazing **PHO**, a fragrant Vietnamese bone-broth soup containing rice noodles, beef, spices, and bean sprouts, and **BANH MI**, a Vietnamese sandwich pairing meat and pickled vegetables on a crusty baguette.

COOL INVENTIONS

• A Seattle waiter named Rob Angel dreamed up the game **PICTIONARY** in 1985. He read the entire dictionary to choose the words!

• Adventurer Eddie Bauer invented the first **PUFFER JACKET** with goose feathers in 1936, after a near-death experience on a winter fishing trip when his wool coat got wet.

BOOKS *The One and Only Ivan* by Katherine Applegate • *Our Only May Amelia* by Jennifer L. Holm

At the ROADKILL COOK-OFF in Marlinton, chefs use dead animals found on the side of the road in tasty dishes. Past winners included "Fender Fried Fawn Smothered in Vulture Vomit" and "Bear Butt Savory Stew."

RAMPS, a wild leek found in forests, are called "little stinkers" because they smell of onion and garlic.

The Clay County GOLDEN DELICIOUS Festival celebrates the yellow apple discovered in the early 1900s.

WOPLD'S LARGEST TEA POT

The world's largest TEAPOT (14 feet high) in Chester started off as a barrel advertising root beer, before a handle and spout were added.

You can't use your hands (or spoons!) at the CHOCOLATE MOUSSE EATING CONTEST at the Lewisburg Chocolate Festival.

Sit in GEORGE WASHINGTON'S BATHTUB in Berkeley Springs State Park, the only outdoor monument to presidential bathing (Washington visited the bubbling mineral springs as a teenager).

MOTHMAN is a mythic half-man, half-moth creature with glowing red eyes and massive wings. After Mothman was reportedly sighted in 1966 in Point Pleasant, the town celebrated the local legend with a statue, museum, and festival!

FAST FACTS

CAPITAL Charleston

FUNNY PLACE NAMES Booger Hole, Cheat Neck, Cucumber, Friendly, Left Hand, Looneyville, Man, Odd, Paw Paw, Pee Wee, Pie, Whirlwind, Wolf Pen

STATE SLANG
• A **HOLLER** has nothing to do with yelling. It's a remote road or area, usually in a valley between mountains.

The **STATE QUARTER** features the **NEW RIVER GORGE BRIDGE**, the longest steel span bridge in the nation. Strangely, the New River is one of the world's oldest rivers, and unusually flows south to north.

WEST VIRGINIA 1863 · NEW RIVER GORGE

FANTASTIC FOODS
• Italian immigrant Giuseppe Argiro created **PEPPERONI ROLLS** (spicy pepperoni baked into a soft, sweet roll) in the 1920s, as a non-perishable lunch for coal miners. Joey Chestnut ate 43 in 10 minutes to break the world record at the 2019 WV Three Rivers Festival.

• **SLAW DOGS** are chili hot dogs topped with creamy, tangy coleslaw. Try this state favorite at the Hot Dog Festival in Huntington.

• **BUCKWHEAT CAKES** are pancakes made with buckwheat flour. Did you know buckwheat is a fruit seed, not a grain?

COOL INVENTIONS
• **MOTHER'S DAY** was started by Anna Jarvis in 1908 in Grafton. She then launched a letter-writing campaign to have it declared a national holiday, pointing out no other holiday celebrated female achievements. President Wilson made it official in 1914.

• Marian McQuade of Oak Hills started **GRANDPARENTS' DAY** in 1973. Forget-me-nots are the official flower of the holiday.

BOOKS *Shiloh* by Phyllis Reynolds Naylor • *Missing May* by Cynthia Rylant

WEST VIRGINIA

The Mountain State

"Almost heaven," is how singer John Denver described West Virginia in his famous anthem "Take Me Home, Country Roads." You'll agree as you swim and paddle in the cool rivers, hike the peaks and valleys, and pitch a tent alongside a blazing campfire. The thickly forested Mountain State lies completely within the Appalachian Mountain range, but here's a head scratcher: is West Virginia the southernmost northern state or the northernmost southern state?

Roll through the National Marble Museum in Weston. The state is the country's biggest producer of GLASS MARBLES.

GRAVE CREEK MOUND is one of the nation's largest prehistoric burial sites, dating back to 250 to 150 BCE. The Adena people moved 60,000 tons of dirt (long before excavators and dump trucks!) to create the 69-foot-tall hill.

In the town of Green Bank, wi-fi, cellphones, cordless speakers, and microwaves are banned to prevent interference with the Green Bank Observatory's powerful TELESCOPES. One of them is the world's largest radio telescope (a college football stadium could fit inside its dish!) that receives messages from the Mars Rover.

JOHN BROWN'S FORT still stands in Harpers Ferry. It's where the famous abolitionist and his followers seized weapons from the armory in 1859, in an attempt to spark a revolt of enslaved people. While unsuccessful, it's believed to have spurred on the Civil War.

The Williamson COAL HOUSE was constructed from 65 tons of coal.

The nation's first BRICK-PAVED STREET was laid in Charleston in 1870.

The world's record for the FASTEST HUMAN WHEELBARROW was set by two medical students in Morgantown, who covered 50 meters in 10.88 seconds in 2020.

State Favorites   COOKIE haystack cookie · VEGETABLE greasy beans · BREAKFAST biscuits and gravy

Say cheese! The average American eats over 40 pounds of cheese per year, and there's a better-than-cheddar chance that most of it came from Wisconsin. The state makes over 600 kinds of cheese, and there are so many cheesy celebrations, including cheese-carving competitions (how about a palace out of provolone?), the Grilled Cheese Championship in Dodgeville, and the Cheese Curd Festival in Ellsworth. Curds—small lumps of cheese collected before it forms into blocks—go squeak when you bite into 'em.

Two Rivers claims the first ICE CREAM SUNDAE was created in their town in 1881, when chocolate syrup was drizzled over ice cream. But Ithaca, NY, says they were first, and the towns' rivalry is known as the "sundae war."

The official bird of Madison is the PLASTIC PINK FLAMINGO.

WISCONSIN

The Badger State

Wisconsin grows more than half of the nation's CRANBERRIES. A cranberry can bounce AND float because it has a small pocket of air inside it.

Head on over to the National BOBBLEHEAD Hall of Fame and Museum in Milwaukee!

The largest WOOLLY MAMMOTH ever excavated was found in Kenosha.

Relish a trip to the National Mustard Museum in Middleton to view the spicy collection of over 6,000 MUSTARDS from all 50 states and over 70 countries.

Like BRAIN TWISTERS? Exercise your mind at the Logic Puzzle Museum in Burlington.

On the outside, the BIG MUSKIE in Haywood looks like an enormous leaping muskellunge fish, but inside is the National Freshwater Fishing Hall of Fame.

State Favorites

DESSERT frozen custard · FUNGI morel mushrooms · PIZZA TOPPING macaroni and cheese

AMERICA'S DAIRYLAND

The record set at the annual Youth Speed Jump Competition in Bloomer, the unofficial JUMP ROPE Capital of the World, is 72 jumps in 10 seconds.

Dozens of wooden TROLLS are scattered about Mount Horeb, the self-declared Troll Capital of the World.

Ta-da! Learn how to escape from "jail" like famous magician HARRY HOUDINI at the History Museum at the Castle in Appleton, the town where he grew up.

Boasting 51 water slides, Noah's Ark in "The Dells" is the largest WATERPARK in the U.S.

The first private American KINDERGARTEN was opened by German immigrant Margarethe Schurz in Watertown in 1856.

Marathon County grows nearly all the GINSENG in the nation. Ginseng root has been used in medicines for centuries by both Native nations and the Chinese.

BRRRR! FRESHWATER SURFERS call Sheboygan the "Malibu of the Midwest." Wear a wetsuit—the waves are highest in Lake Michigan when snow's on the ground.

The world's largest PENNY (15 feet high) in Woodruff honors students who collected over 1.7 million pennies in 1953 to help build the community hospital.

FAST FACTS

CAPITAL Madison

FUNNY PLACE NAMES Avalanche, Chili, Disco, Egg Harbor, Embarrass, Fence, Footville, Moose Junction, New Diggings, Random Lake

STATE SLANG

Feeling thirsty? Find a BUBBLER (a water fountain).

Cheese-lovin' Wisconsinites and Green Bay Packers fans are called CHEESEHEADS. Ralph Bruno created the first wedge cheesehead hat in 1987, with foam pulled out of his mom's couch.

The **STATE QUARTER** features a cow, a round of cheese, and an ear of corn. With over a million cows, Wisconsin is known as AMERICA'S DAIRYLAND.

FANTASTIC FOODS

The KRINGLE, introduced by Danish immigrants in the 1800s, is an oval-shaped, flaky pastry stuffed with fruit, nuts, or cream cheese. Racine is the nation's kringle capital.

BRATWURST is a German-style sausage that's often brushed with melted butter. Sheboygan is advertised as the Bratwurst Capital of the World.

Festivals all over the state serve BOOYAH, a slow-simmering, everything-but-the-kitchen-sink stew of meat and vegetables.

COOL INVENTIONS

On the first TYPEWRITER to be a commercial success, invented by Christopher Latham Sholes of Milwaukee in 1867, the keyboard was alphabetical. But when nearby keys were hit at the same time, they jammed. Sholes rearranged the keys so the letters most commonly used were away from each other. His QWERTY keyboard is still on computers and cell phones today.

AMERICAN GIRL dolls were invented by Pleasant Rowland in Middleton.

BOOKS *The Westing Game* by Ellen Raskin
Hope Was Here by Joan Bauer

The first DUDE RANCH (guest ranch) was opened by the Eatons family in North Dakota then moved to Wyoming in 1904. Back then, "dude" was the name for a pampered visitor, usually from an East coast city.

The North Antelope Rochelle coal mine in the Powder River Basin is the world's largest COAL MINE, with an estimated 1.7 billion tons of recoverable coal.

There are only two ESCALATORS in the entire state, both in Casper.

Wyoming is one of only three states with a name beginning with TWO CONSONANTS. (Florida and Rhode Island are the other two.)

A Casper fifth-grade class discovered the bones of a CAMARASAURUS during a field trip in Alcova.

OLD FAITHFUL, a geyser in Yellowstone National Park, shoots up scalding-hot water every 60–110 minutes. In the early 1800s, some people used the geyser as a washing machine, throwing their clothes in between eruptions and waiting for them to be shot back out. Today, we know better: throwing things inside the geyser destroys it.

Harry Longabaugh became known as the SUNDANCE KID, because he served a jail term for horse-stealing in the town of Sundance.

FAST FACTS

CAPITAL Cheyenne

FUNNY PLACE NAMES Burntfork, Chugwater, Dad, Dull Center, Frannie, Jay Em, Lost Cabin, Muddy Gap, Saddlestring, Ten Sleep, West Thumb

STATE SLANG

• A **GULLY WASHER** is a quick, heavy rain.

• A **COUPLE TWO THREE** means a few, as in, "I overslept a couple two three times this month."

• If you're riding a horse, **"HOLD TIGHT TO THE BRISKET"** means grab on to the saddle horn.

The **STATE QUARTER** features a bucking horse and rider. Many say the horse is **STEAMBOAT**, the famous bucking bronco with the nickname "horse that couldn't be ridden." The black gelding's stubbornness and energy represent the spirit of Wyoming.

WYOMING 1890 THE EQUALITY STATE

FANTASTIC FOODS

• **ELK JERKY STICKS** are strips of elk meat that have been dried and seasoned.

• Cast your line! Wyoming overflows with trout streams and rivers, so **PAN-FRIED TROUT** appears on many menus. The official state fish is the cutthroat trout.

• **CHOKECHERRY JAM** is made from the tart, purple-black wild fruits that are also called "bitter berries."

COOL INVENTIONS

• The first **J.C. PENNEY** store was opened in Kemmerer by James Cash Penney in 1902.

BOOKS *Paint the Wind* by Pam Muñoz Ryan • *The Haymeadow* by Gary Paulsen

In 2006, at age 88, Wyoming native Bob Champion (perfect last name!) became the oldest winner of a class championship at the World HORSESHOE PITCHERS TOURNAMENT in Gillette.

Wyoming, then a territory, was the first state to grant WOMEN THE RIGHT TO VOTE in 1869 (that's how it got the nickname the "Equality State"), and the first to elect a female governor in 1925.

The Museum of Flight and Aerial Firefighting in Greybull honors the brave people who've battled raging FOREST FIRES from the air.

The Equality State
WYOMING

THE COWBOY STATE

Rodeo has been a part of Wyoming's western heritage and rugged landscape for over a century. Crowds fill the stands at the Cody Stampede Rodeo and at the Frontier Days celebration in Cheyenne, billed as the world's largest outdoor rodeo. They cheer for bull riders, who try to stay on a 1,800-pound bucking bull for eight seconds (way longer than it seems!) with one arm in the air and without letting go of a rope. Kids can also get a turn—but on a mechanical or inflatable bull. Hold on! It's a bumpy ride on these bucking machines . . .

FOSSIL CABIN near Medicine Bow was built in 1932 from rocks containing over 5,700 dinosaur fossils.

A 75-foot arch made out of over 3,000 ELK ANTLERS hangs over Afton's main street. Only male elk, or bulls, have antlers, which grow in the spring and fall off, or shed, each winter.

In 1939, ranchers in northern Wyoming, South Dakota, and Montana tried (unsuccessfully) to form a new state called ABSAROKA, from the Crow word meaning "children of the large-beaked bird."

History left its mark! Names and dates that travelers on the OREGON TRAIL carved into Register Cliff, Names Hill, and Independence Rock are still there. In the 1800s, wagon trains tried to reach Independence Rock by July 4th in order to make it to the West Coast before first snowfall.

State Favorites   CANDY malted milk balls · SNACK Taco John's potato olés · PIZZA TOPPING pepperoni

Why is Washington, D.C. a city and not a state? The nation's founders wrote into the Constitution that the U.S. capital couldn't be a state, because they were afraid of giving one state so much power. Today, over 700,000 people live in D.C. (more than both Wyoming and Vermont!). They want representation in the country's government and have been trying to overturn the law. If Washington, D.C. becomes the 51st state, D.C.—which stands for the District of Columbia (after Christopher Columbus)—would probably be switched to "Douglass Commonwealth" to honor abolitionist Frederick Douglass.

John Adams—not George Washington—was the first president to call the WHITE HOUSE home. The White House has a movie theater, bowling alley, flower shop, dentist office, and swimming pool!

The LIBRARY OF CONGRESS—the largest library in the U.S. with more than 170 million items and 838 miles of bookshelves—has a teeny-tiny book the size of the period at the end of this sentence.

WASHINGTON, D.C.

The Nation's Capital

Can you spell "scherenschnitte?" Show off your mad spelling skills at the annual Scripps National SPELLING BEE. (To save you a trip to the dictionary: scherenschnitte is the art of cutting paper into decorative designs—such as paper snowflakes.)

Hundreds of Barbie dolls in holiday or politically inspired outfits are arranged around the BARBIE POND on Avenue Q.

SOAPMAN, a mummified man from the 1800s, is at the Smithsonian's Museum of Natural History. Alkaline water from the soil seeped into his casket and created a chemical reaction with his body fat—changing it to soap!

In 1912, the mayor of Tokyo, Japan, sent a gift of 3,000 CHERRY TREES to Washington, D.C. Today, thousands of the fragrant trees surround the Tidal Basin. But be warned—it's against the law to pick a CHERRY BLOSSOM flower!

All the dollar bills in your piggy bank were created at the Bureau of ENGRAVING AND PRINTING.

Go undercover at the International SPY MUSEUM, where a secret world of espionage and cool gadgets like itty-bitty buttonhole cameras await.

See YOUR FACE ON A POSTAGE STAMP at the Smithsonian National Postal Museum.

STATE Favorites DESSERT cupcake • PIZZA TOPPING pepperoni • SNACK Salvadoran pupusas

Supersized! The District's jumbo PIZZA SLICES can be over 15 inches long!

Visit all 50 STATES in an annual bike ride along every state-named avenue (62 miles!). Or pedal the much-shorter 13 Colonies Ride.

A tree that whispers in over 100 different languages stands at PLANET WORD, a museum about language.

A gargoyle of Star Wars villain DARTH VADER looms on the outer wall of the Washington National Cathedral. Inside, a MOON ROCK collected by Apollo 11 astronauts during the 1969 first moon walk is at the center of a stained-glass window, called the Space Window.

Dr. Martin Luther King Jr. gave his famous "I HAVE A DREAM" speech in front of nearly 250,000 people at the Lincoln Memorial in 1963. However, the "dream" part wasn't originally in the speech—he added it after his friend Mahalia Jackson, a gospel singer, called out: "Tell 'em about the dream, Martin."

At 555 feet, the WASHINGTON MONUMENT is the world's tallest obelisk. A time capsule containing copies of the Declaration of Independence and the Constitution is buried in one of the cornerstones.

FAST FACTS

CAPITAL OF THE UNITED STATES

FUNNY PLACE NAMES
Capitalsaurus Court, Chevy Chase, Foggy Bottom, Outlaw Way, Quackenbos Street, Unicorn Lane

STATE SLANG
• The **MALL** isn't a shopping mall—it's the National Mall, a park containing the Lincoln Memorial, U.S. Capitol, Smithsonian museums, and other monuments and memorials.

• The **HILL** is Capitol Hill, where Congress meets.

• The **BELTWAY** is a highway that circles the city like a belt.

The **STATE QUARTER** features the great composer, bandleader, and **JAZZ** musician **DUKE ELLINGTON**, who was born in the District and received the Presidential Medal of Freedom and the Grammy Lifetime Achievement Award. At age 15, he had a job at a soda fountain and wrote his first song, "Soda Fountain Rag."

FANTASTIC FOODS
• Half-smoked, half-grilled spicy pork and beef sausages are called **HALF-SMOKES**.

• D.C.-ites tear off pieces of **INJERA**, a round, spongy flatbread from Ethiopia, and use them to scoop up vegetable or meat stews. D.C. is home to one of the nation's largest Ethiopian populations.

• Red-orange, sweet-and-sour **MUMBO SAUCE** (or mambo sauce) is enjoyed on fried foods.

COOL INVENTIONS
• Surgeon Dr. Charles Drew created **BLOOD BANKS** during World War II, helping to save thousands of lives. At a blood bank, blood is collected, tested, sorted by type, and stored to be used for transfusions.

BOOKS Spirit Hunters by Ellen Oh • The Worst Class Trip Ever by Dave Barry

INDEX

The names, trademarks, and logos of the named entities and brands profiled in this book are the property of their respective owners and are used solely for identification purposes. This book is a publication of Quarto Publishing plc and it has not been prepared, approved, endorsed, or licensed by any other brand, person, or entity.

To Rachel Minay—I couldn't have done this without you!—HA

Author Acknowledgments

Special thanks to Lucy Brownridge and the talented Myrto Dimitrakoulia, as well as Elise McMullan-Ciotti, Marlo Alexander, Brein Lopez, Sharon Hearn, and the amazing booksellers at Children's Book World in Los Angeles. And big thanks to the librarians throughout the country. The best way to find out anything and everything? **Ask a librarian!**

Text © 2021 Heather Alexander L.L.C. Illustrations © 2021 Alan Berry Rhys

First published in 2021 by Wide Eyed Editions, an imprint of The Quarto Group.
First published in paperback in 2024 by Wide Eyed Editions.
100 Cummings Center, Suite 265D, Beverly, MA 01915, USA.
T +1 978-282-9590 **www.Quarto.com**

A CIP record for this book is available from the Library of Congress.

ISBN 978-0-7112-9321-2
eISBN 978-0-7112-6811-1

The illustrations were created digitally
Set in Quicksand and Vibur

Published by Georgia Amson-Bradshaw
Designed by Myrto Dimitrakoulia
Commissioned by Lucy Brownridge
Edited by Rachel Minay
Edited for paperback by Claire Saunders
Editorial assistance from Alex Hithersay
Production by Dawn Cameron

Manufactured in Guangdong, China TT012024

9 8 7 6 5 4 3 2 1